Test Yourself

Personality and İndividual Differences

Test Yourself... Psychology Series

Test Yourself: Biological Psychology ISBN 978 0 85725 649 2

Test Yourself: Cognitive Psychology ISBN 978 0 85725 669 0

Test Yourself: Developmental Psychology ISBN 978 0 85725 657 7

Test Yourself: Personality and Individual Differences ISBN 978 0 85725 661 4

Test Yourself: Research Methods and Design in Psychology ISBN 978 0 85725 665 2

Test Yourself: Social Psychology ISBN 978 0 85725 653 9

Test Yourself

Personality and İndividual Differences

Dominic Upton and Penney Upton

Multiple-Choice Questions prepared by Daniel Kay

LearningMatters

First published in 2011 by Learning Matters Ltd

British Library Cataloguing in Publication Data
A CIP record for this book is available from the British Library

ISBN: 978 0 85725 661 4

This book is also available in the following e-book formats:
Adobe ebook ISBN: 978 0 85725 663 8
ePUB book ISBN: 978 0 85725 662 1
Kindle ISBN: 978 0 85725 664 5

Cover design by Toucan Design
Text design by Toucan Design
Project Management by Deer Park Productions, Tavistock, Devon
Typeset by Pantek Media, Maidstone, Kent
Printed and bound in Great Britain by Bell & Bain Ltd, Glasgow

Learning Matters Ltd
20 Cathedral Yard
Exeter
EX1 1HB
Tel: 01392 215560
info@learningmatters.co.uk
www.learningmatters.co.uk

Contents

Acknowledgements

The production of this series has been a rapid process with an apparent deadline at almost every turn. We are therefore grateful to colleagues both from Learning Matters (Julia Morris and Helen Fairlie) and the University of Worcester for making this process so smooth and (relatively) effortless. In particular we wish to thank our colleagues for providing many of the questions, specifically:

- Biological Psychology: Emma Preece
- Cognitive Psychology: Emma Preece
- Developmental Psychology: Charlotte Taylor
- Personality and Individual Differences: Daniel Kay
- Research Methods and Design in Psychology: Laura Scurlock-Evans
- Social Psychology: Laura Scurlock-Evans

Finally, we must, once again, thank our children (Gabriel, Rosie and Francesca) for not being as demanding as usual during the process of writing and development.

Introduction

Psychology is one of the most exciting subjects that you can study at university in the twenty-first century. A degree in psychology helps you to understand and explain thought, emotion and behaviour. You can then apply this knowledge to a range of issues in everyday life including health and well-being, performance in the workplace, education – in fact any aspect of life you can think of! However, a degree in psychology gives you much more than a set of 'facts' about mind and behaviour; it will also equip you with a wide range of skills and knowledge. Some of these, such as critical thinking and essay writing, have much in common with humanities subjects, while others such as hypothesis testing and numeracy are scientific in nature. This broad-based skill set prepares you exceptionally well for the workplace – whether or not your chosen profession is in psychology. Indeed, recent evidence suggests employers appreciate the skills and knowledge of psychology graduates. A psychology degree really can help you get ahead of the crowd. However, in order to reach this position of excellence, you need to develop your skills and knowledge fully and ensure you complete your degree to your highest ability.

This book is designed to enable you, as a psychology student, to maximise your learning potential by assessing your level of understanding and your confidence and competence in personality and individual differences, one of the core knowledge domains for psychology. It does this by providing you with essential practice in the types of questions you will encounter in your formal university assessments. It will also help you make sense of your results and identify your strengths and weaknesses. This book is one part of a series of books designed to assist you with learning and developing your knowledge of psychology. The series includes books on:

- Biological Psychology
- Cognitive Psychology
- Developmental Psychology
- Personality and Individual Differences
- Research Methods and Design in Psychology
- Social Psychology

In order to support your learning this book includes over 200 targeted Multiple-Choice Questions (MCQs) and Extended Multiple-Choice Questions (EMCQs) that have been carefully put together to help assess your depth of knowledge of personality and individual differences. The MCQs are split into two formats: the foundation level questions are about your level of understanding of the key principles and components of key areas in psychology. Hopefully, within these questions you should recognise the correct answer from the four options. The advanced level questions require more than simple recognition – some will require recall of key information, some will require application of this information and others will require synthesis of information. At the end of each chapter you will find a set of essay questions covering each of the topics. These are typical of the kinds of question that you are likely to encounter during your studies. In each chapter, the first essay question is broken down for you using a concept map, which is intended to help you develop a detailed answer to the question. Each of the concept maps is shaded to show you how topics link together, and includes cross-references to relevant MCQs in the chapter. You should be able to see a progression in your learning from the foundation to the advanced MCQs, to the extended MCQs and finally the essay questions. The book is divided up into 9 chapters and your personality and individual differences module is likely to have been divided into similar topic areas. However, do not let this restrict your thinking in relation to personality and individual differences: these topics interact. The sample essay questions, which complement the questions provided in the chapter, will help you to make the links between different topic areas. You will find the answers to all of the MCQs and EMCQs at the end of the book. There is a separate table of answers for each chapter; use the self monitoring column in each of the tables to write down your own results, coding correct answers as NC, incorrect answers as NI and any you did not respond to as NR. You can then use the table on page 91 to analyse your results.

The aim of the book is not only to help you revise for your exams, it is also intended to help with your learning. However, it is not intended to replace lectures, seminars and tutorials, or to supersede the book chapters and journal articles signposted by your lecturers. What this book can do, however, is set you off on a sound footing for your revision and preparation for your exams. In order to help you to consolidate your learning, the book also contains tips on how to approach MCQ assessments and how you can use the material in this text to assess, *and enhance*, your knowledge base and level of understanding.

Now you know the reasons behind this book and how it will enhance your success, it is time for you to move on to the questions – let the fun begin!

Assessing your interest, competence and confidence

The aim of this book is to help you to maximise your learning potential by assessing your level of understanding, confidence and competence in core issues in psychology. So how does it do this?

Assessing someone's knowledge of a subject through MCQs might at first glance seem fairly straightforward: typically the MCQ consists of a question, one correct answer and one or more incorrect answers, sometimes called distractors. For example, in this book each question has one right answer and three distractors. The goal of an MCQ test is for you to get every question right and so show just how much knowledge you have. However, because you are given a number of answers to select from, you might be able to choose the right answer either by guessing or by a simple process of elimination – in other words by knowing what is not the right answer. For this reason it is sometimes argued that MCQs only test knowledge of facts rather than in-depth understanding of a subject. However, there is increasing evidence that MCQs can also be valuable at a much higher level of learning, if used in the right way (see, for example, Gardner-Medwin and Gahan, 2003). They can help you to develop as a self-reflective learner who is able to recognise the interest you have in a subject matter as well as your level of competence and confidence in your own knowledge.

MCQs can help you gauge your interest, competence and confidence in the following way. It has been suggested (Howell, 1982) that there are four possible states of knowledge (see Table 1). Firstly, it is possible that you do not know something and are not aware of this lack of knowledge. This describes the naive learner – think back to your first week at university when you were a 'fresher' student and had not yet begun your psychology course. Even if you had done psychology at A level, you were probably feeling a little self-conscious and uncertain in this new learning environment. During the first encounter in a new learning situation most of us feel tentative and unsure of ourselves; this is because we don't yet know what it is we don't know – although to feel this lack of certainty suggests that we know there is something we don't know, even if we don't yet know what this is! In contrast, some people appear to be confident and at ease even in new learning situations; this is not usually because they already know everything but rather because they too do not yet know what it is they do not know – but they have yet to even acknowledge that there is a gap in their knowledge. The next step on from this 'unconscious non-competence' is 'conscious non-competence'; once you started your psychology course you began to realise what the gaps were in your knowledge – you now knew what you didn't know! While this can be an uncomfortable feeling, it is important for the learning process that this acknowledgement of a gap in knowledge is made, because it is the first step in reaching the next level of learning – that of a 'conscious competent' learner. In other words you need to know what the gap in your knowledge is so that you can fill it.

Table 1 Consciousness and competence in learning

	Unconscious	Conscious
Non-competent	You don't know something and are not aware that you lack this knowledge/skill.	You don't know something and are aware that you lack this knowledge/skill.
Competent	You know something but are not aware of your knowledge/skill.	You know something and are aware of your knowledge/skill.

One of the ways this book can help you move from unconscious non-competency to conscious competency should by now be clear – it can help you identify the gaps in your knowledge. However, if used properly it can do much more; it can also help you to assess your consciousness and competence in this knowledge.

When you answer an MCQ, you will no doubt have a feeling about how confident you are about your answer: 'I know the answer to question 1 is A. Question 2 I am not so sure about. I am certain the answer is not C or D, so it must be A or B. Question 3, I haven't got a clue so I will say D – but that is a complete guess.' Sound familiar? Some questions you know the answers to, you have that knowledge and know you have it; other questions you are less confident about but think you may know which (if not all) are the distractors, while for others you know this is something you just don't know. Making use of this feeling of confidence will help you become a more reflective – and therefore effective – learner.

Perhaps by now you are wondering where we are going with this and how any of this can help you learn. 'Surely all that matters is whether or not I get the answers right? Does that show I have knowledge?' Indeed it may well do and certainly, if you are confident in your answers, then yes it does. But what if you were not sure? What if your guess of D for our fictional question 3 above was correct? What if you were able to complete all the MCQs in a test and score enough to pass – but every single answer was a guess? Do you really know and understand psychology because you have performed well – and will you be able to do the same again if you retake the test next week? Take a look back at Table 1. If you are relying on guesswork and hit upon the answer by accident you might perform well without actually understanding how you know the answer, or that you even knew it (unconscious competence), or you may not realise you don't know something (unconscious non-competence). According to this approach to using MCQs what is important is not how many answers you get right, but whether or not you acknowledge your confidence in the answer you give: it is better to get a wrong answer and acknowledge it is wrong (so as to work on filling that gap).

Therefore what we recommend you do when completing the MCQs is this: for each answer you give, think about how confident you are that it is right. You might want to rate each of your answers on the following scale:

3:   I am confident this is the right answer.

2:   I am not sure, but I think this is the right answer.

1:   I am not sure, but I think this is the wrong answer.

0:   I am confident this is the wrong answer.

Using this system of rating your confidence will help you learn for yourself both what you know and what you don't know. You will become a conscious learner through the self-directed activities contained in this book. Reflection reinforces the links between different areas of your learning and knowledge and strengthens your ability to *justify* an answer, so enabling you to perform to the best of your ability.

References

Gardner-Medwin, A.R. and Gahan, M. (2003) *Formative and Summative Confidence-Based Assessment*, Proceedings of 7th International Computer-Aided Assessment Conference, Loughborough, UK, July, pp. 147–55.

Howell, W.C. (1982) 'An overview of models, methods, and problems', in W.C. Howell and E.A. Fleishman (eds), *Human performance and productivity, Vol. 2: Information processing and decision making*. Hillsdale, NJ: Erlbaum.

Tips for success: how to succeed in your assessments

This book, part of a comprehensive new series, will help you achieve your psychology aspirations. It is designed to assess your knowledge so that you can review your current level of performance and where you need to spend more time and effort reviewing and revising material. However, it hopes to do more than this – it aims to assist you with your learning so it not only acts as an assessor of performance but as an aid to learning. Obviously, it is not a replacement for every single text, journal article, presentation and abstract you will read and review during the course of your degree programme. Similarly, it is in no way a replacement for your lectures, seminars or additional reading – it should complement all of this material. However, it will also add something to all of this other material: learning is assisted by reviewing and assessing and this is what this text aims to do – help you learn through assessing your learning.

The focus throughout this book, as it is in all of the books in this series, is on how you should approach and consider your topics in relation to assessment and exams. Various features have been included to help you build up your skills and knowledge ready for your assessments.

This book, and the other companion volumes in this series, should help you learn through testing and assessing yourself – it should provide an indication of how advanced your thinking and understanding is. Once you have assessed your understanding you can explore what you need to learn and how. However, hopefully, quite a bit of what you read here you will already have come across and the text will act as a reminder and set your mind at rest – you do know your material.

Succeeding at MCQs

Exams based on MCQs are becoming more and more frequently used in higher education and particularly in psychology. As such you need to know the best strategy for completing such assessments and succeeding. The first thing to note is, if you know the material then the questions will present no problems – so revise and understand your notes and back this up with in-depth review of material presented in textbooks, specialist materials and journal articles. However, once you have done this you need to look at the technique for answering multiple-choice questions and here are some tips for success:

1. Time yourself. The first important thing to note when you are sitting your examination is the time available to you for completing it. If you have, for example, an hour and a half to answer 100 multiple-choice questions this means you have 54 seconds to complete each question. This means that you have to read, interpret, think about and select one answer for a multiple-choice question in under a minute. This may seem impossible, but there are several things that you can do to use your time effectively.

2. Practise. By using the examples in this book, those given out in your courses, in class tests, or on the web you can become familiar with the format and wording of multiple-choice questions similar to those used in your exam. Another way of improving your chances is to set your own multiple-choice exams – try and think of some key questions and your four optional responses (including the correct one of course!). Try and think of optional distractors that are sensible and not completely obvious. You could, of course, swap questions with your peers – getting them to set some questions for you while you set some questions for them. Not only will this help you with your practice but you will also understand the format of MCQs and the principles underlying their construction – this will help you answer the questions when it comes to the real thing.

3. The rule of totality. Look out for words like 'never' and 'always' in multiple-choice questions. It is rare in psychology for any answer to be true in relation to these words of 'totality'. As we all know, psychology is a multi-modal subject that has multiple perspectives and conflicting views and so it is very unlikely that there will always be a 'never' or an 'always'. When you see these words, focus on them and consider them carefully. A caveat is, of course, sometimes never and always will appear in a question, but be careful of these words!

4. Multiple, multiple-choice answers. Some multiple-choice answers will contain statements such as 'both A and C' or 'all of the above' or 'none of these'. Do not be distracted by these choices. Multiple-choice questions have only one correct answer and do not ask for opinion or personal bias. Quickly go through each choice independently, crossing off the answers that you know are not true. If, after eliminating the incorrect responses, you think there is more than one correct answer, group your answers and see if one of the choices matches yours. If you believe only one answer is correct, do not be distracted by multiple-choice possibilities.

5. 'First guess is best' fallacy. There is a myth among those who take (or even write) MCQs that the 'first guess is best'. This piece of folklore is misleading: research (and psychologists love research) indicates that when people change their answers on an MCQ exam, about two-thirds of the time they go from wrong to right, showing that the first guess is often not the best. So, think about it and consider your answer – is it right? Remember, your first guess is not better than a result obtained through good, hard, step-by-step, conscious thinking that enables you to select the answer that you believe to be the best.

6. The rule of threes. One of the most helpful strategies for multiple-choice questions is a three-step process:

(i)   Read the question thoroughly but quickly. Concentrate on particular words such as 'due to' and 'because' or 'as a result of' and on words of totality such as 'never' or 'always' (although see rule 3 above).

(ii)   Rather than going to the first answer you think is correct (see rule 5) eliminate the ones that you think are wrong one by one. While this may take more time, it is more likely to provide the correct answer. Furthermore, answer elimination may provide a clue to a misread answer you may have overlooked.

(iii) Reread the question, as if you were reading it for the first time. Now choose your answer from your remaining answers based on this rereading.

7. Examine carefully. Examine each of the questions carefully, particularly those that are very similar. It may be that exploring parts of the question will be useful – circle the parts that are different. It is possible that each of the alternatives will be very familiar and hence you must **understand the meaning** of each of the alternatives with respect to the context of the question. You can achieve this by studying for the test as though it will be a short-answer or essay test. Look for the level of **qualifying words**. Such words as *best, always, all, no, never, none, entirely, completely* suggest that a condition exists without exception. Items containing words that provide for some level of exception or qualification are: *often, usually, less, seldom, few, more* and *most* (and see rule 3). If you know that two or three of the options are correct, **'all of the above'** is a strong possibility.

8. Educated guesses. Never leave a question unanswered. If nothing looks familiar, pick the answer that seems most complete and contains the most information. Most of the time (if not all of the time!) the best way to answer a question is to know the answer! However, there may be times when you will not know the answer or will not really understand the question. There are three circumstances in which you should guess: when you are stuck, when you are running out of time, or both of these! Guessing strategies are always dependent on the scoring system used to mark the exam (see the section on MCQ scoring mechanisms). If the multiple-choice scoring system makes the odds of gaining points equal to the odds of having points deducted it does not pay to guess if you are unable to eliminate any of the answers. But the odds of improving your test score are in your favour if you can rule out even one of the answers. The odds in your favour increase as you rule out more answers in any one question. So, take account of the scoring mechanisms and then eliminate, move onwards and guess!

9. Revise and learn. Study carefully and learn your material. The best tip for success is always to learn the material. Use this book, use your material, use your time wisely but, most of all, use your brain!

Chapter 1
Individual differences psychology: an introduction

This chapter provides questions relating to individual differences psychology. Topics include how individual differences psychology is distinguishable from other psychological areas such as cognitive, developmental and educational, the aims of individual-differences psychology, the way measures are employed and ethical practicalities.

Select one of the possible answers for each question.

Foundation level questions

1. Which of the following is a context for which individual differences psychology does not have a major application?

   A. Education.

   B. Occupation (work).

   C. Criminal justice system.

   D. Astrobiology.

   Your answer: [ ]

2. Which of the following is not a feature of individual differences psychology?

   A. Description of enduring characteristics or dispositions.

   B. Investigation of the determinants – or the causes – of individual differences.

   C. Attempts to study perceived and experienced individual differences.

   D. A central focus on the behaviour of *Big Brother* winners.

   Your answer: [ ]

3. Currently, what is the predominant approach to the measurement of individual differences?

A. Psychodynamic.

B. Psychometric.

C. Idiographic.

D. Nomothetic.

Your answer: ☐

4. Broadly, what does psychometrics mean in terms of individual differences psychology?

A. Measurement of habit formation and stimulus response.

B. Measurement of personality determinants via non-numeric data.

C. Measurement of observable individual differences that are turned into numerical data.

D. Measurement of random events.

Your answer: ☐

5. What is a key assumption of the psychometric approach?

A. Groups can be compared with individuals.

B. Individuals are similar.

C. Individuals and groups are different.

D. Scaling represents real differences in the physical world.

Your answer: ☐

6. At present, which from the list below is a consequence of the psychometric approach?

A. Research is focused (primarily) toward the causes of individual differences.

B. Research focuses (in the main) on the nature and structure of individual differences.

C. Research is focused (primarily) on how individual differences function.

D. Largely focuses research toward the purpose of individual differences.

Your answer: ☐

7. Which of the following is an advantage of the application of the scientific method to individual differences?

   A. Increases people's belief in individual differences.

   B. More accurate predictions of human variation.

   C. Promotes the popularity of the subject.

   D. Popularises the scientific method.

Your answer: ☐

Advanced level questions

8. From the options below, how is the nomothetic approach different to the idiographic?

   A. The nomothetic approach describes the way an individual varies within themselves.

   B. The nomothetic approach describes intra-individual variation.

   C. The nomothetic approach is a non-numerical approach.

   D. The nomothetic approach only describes how groups differ on a particular individual difference.

Your answer: ☐

9. What does the 'accessibility debate' refer to?

   A. The difficulty in finding a representative sample.

   B. How accessible certain individual difference tests are to the public.

   C. The disagreement of how enduring dispositions are accessible or observable directly.

   D. The agreement of how accessible or observable directly enduring dispositions are.

Your answer: ☐

10. Which of the following groups includes four types of data used within individual differences research?

A. S-Data, O-Data, L-Data and T-Data.

B. R-Data, A-Data, Z-Data and X-Data.

C. ZZ-Data, RX-Data, PT-Data and AA-Data.

D. L-Data, V-Data, O-Data and A-Data.

Your answer: ☐

11. What is one disadvantage to employing O-Data?

A. O-Data does not produce numerical data.

B. O-Data methods are the same as S-Data methods and succumb to the same biases.

C. O-Data cannot be collected by using a standardised method.

D. Possible observer biases in the interpretation of other people's behaviour.

Your answer: ☐

12. According to Bartram and Lindley (2005), what is maximum performance?

A. A measure of personality.

B. A measure of motivation or 'drive'.

C. A measure of beliefs and values.

D. The outcome in an assessment of what people *can do* in terms of attainment, ability and aptitude.

13. Why, at times, is it difficult to interpret the term *individual's* data in individual differences psychology?

A. It is unknown which *individuals* are included in the data.

B. Because *individual's* refers to more than one person.

C. The term encompasses the sum of individual differences of one person.

D. The term refers to *aggregate* data that is the sum of the mean or composite scores of other individuals or groups.

Your answer: ☐

14. Which research design on individual differences is currently used most often?

   A. Experimental.

   B. Correlational.

   C. Observational.

   D. None of the above.

Your answer: ☐

15. Which of the following is an assumption underlying the self-report method?

   A. Responses are unlikely to be biased.

   B. Responses provide meaningful numerical information about individuals.

   C. Responses provide meaningful qualitative data about individuals.

   D. The researcher might know the respondent personally.

Your answer: ☐

16.   What does test data assess?

   A. Individual typical performance.

   B. Individual performance.

   C. Individual maximum performance.

   D. Group performance.

Your answer: ☐

17. Why are accurate self-report inventories challenging to develop?

   A. Because no methods have yet been developed to ensure self-report inventories are accurate.

   B. Because response bias provides challenges for researchers to make valid and reliable inventories.

   C. Because reliability and validity cannot be used when designing self-report inventories.

   D. None of the above.

Your answer: ☐

18. Which of the following is an advantage to self-report inventories?

A. Self-report inventories provide a comparative standard with other members of a population.

B. It is relatively simple to construct a reliable measure through self-report methods.

C. It takes longer to construct self-reports than it does for people to respond to them.

D. Relatively low cost to produce making them a more valid method of data collection.

Your answer: ☐

19. For what main reason is it important to make a test or inventory reliable?

A. To challenge psychologists.

B. To be consistent in the collection of *true scores* or scores as near to their *true score* as possible.

C. To prevent biased responding.

D. To make sure the test or inventory measures what it intends to measure.

Your answer: ☐

20. How can we maximise the reliability of an individual differences inventory or test?

A. Increase random error and reduce systematic error.

B. Reduce random error and increase systematic error.

C. Reduce random and systematic error by a solution called *domain sampling*.

D. Increase both random and systematic error.

Your answer: ☐

21. Why is it important to be careful how the data from individual differences tests are used?

A. Because of the ethical implications for decisions made, based on this information.

B. Tests can be used as a 'mark' of status by comparing scores.

C. The government will manipulate your life chances based on your scores.

D. It does not matter how data from individual differences tests are used.

Your answer: ☐

22. Which of the following groups are all types of reliability?

    A. Test retest, alpha coefficient, inter-rater.

    B. Domain sampling, test retest, self-reports.

    C. Test retest, alpha coefficients, self-reports.

    D. Alpha coefficients, domain sampling, self-reports.

Your answer: ☐

23. Why is access to many individual differences tests restricted?

    A. Because many people do not understand the tests.

    B. They are a secret only for psychologists to use.

    C. Because they include vulnerable groups.

    D. It is an attempt to reduce the misuse and abuse of measurements.

Your answer: ☐

24. Which of the following best describes how people manage themselves in different life domains?

    A. Self-regulation.

    B. People-regulation.

    C. Peer-regulation.

    D. Adult-regulation.

Your answer: ☐

25. Which of the following is not a type of validity?

    A. Face.

    B. Construct.

    C. Convergent.

    D. Diverse.

Your answer: ☐

26. Why might scientists be wary of instruments that possess high face validity?

A. Because face validity does not ensure an instrument accurately assesses what it claims to.

B. Because face validity is a heuristic and not a hard and fast rule.

C. Because face validity is not a measure of validity.

D. Scientists do not fully understand what face validity is.

Your answer: ☐

Extended multiple-choice question

Complete the following paragraph using the items listed below and opposite. Not all items can be used because not all items will be consistent with the paragraph. Items can only be used once.

The scientific measurement of _____ dispositions is a predominant focus within the field of individual-differences psychology. This is partly because _____ or characteristics that typify people are assumed to represent meaning and therefore have consequences for individuals and groups. A feature of this _____ approach is it provides scientists with a_____ _____ with other members of the population, which can be applied through valid and _____ instruments. However, scoring and interpretation are complex, and include ethical as well as development and _____ challenges in the application of individual-differences measures. Consequently, a call for an _____ approach to individual differences has been made as part of an effort to consolidate a whole-person approach to the field.

Optional items

A. enduring

B. behaviour

C. dispositions

D. randomised

E. systematic

F. comparative standard

G. normative standard

H. reliable

I. unreliable

J. integrated

K. psychoanalytic

L. cognitive

M. administrative

N. selective

Essay questions for Chapter 1

Once you have completed the MCQs above you should be ready to tackle some essay questions. You might like to select three or four topics and make notes on them. One way to do this is to create a concept map. The concept map for the first question has been done for you and you can see how the knowledge required links to some of the MCQs in this chapter.

1. 'Enduring dispositions are accessible or observable directly.' To what extent do you agree with this view?

2. Identify and critically assess two methods used to collect personality data.

3. Critically evaluate how psychologists measure individual differences and personality.

4. Why is it important not only to consider but also to apply 'good' ethical practice in the complex interpretation of individual differences test scores? Illustrate your answer with relevant examples.

5. Critically evaluate the usefulness of making measures of personality as accurate as possible.

6. Discuss the difficulties associated with defining individual differences.

7. Outline and discuss the main criteria that can be used to evaluate individual differences theories.

8. Critically evaluate the self-report inventory approach to the collection of individual differences data.

Chapter 1 essay question 1: concept map

'Enduring dispositions are accessible or observable directly'. To what extent do you agree with this view?

The concept map below provides an example of how the first sample essay may be conceptualised. Consideration of the scientific approach to individual differences psychology leads to several sub-topics, which can be critically evaluated before conclusions can be drawn. In this case the evidence suggests dispositions are to a certain extent observable; however, interpretations of the data are complex. Therefore enduring dispositions must not be oversimplified. Remember that it is important to link your answers to other topic areas not covered in this chapter.

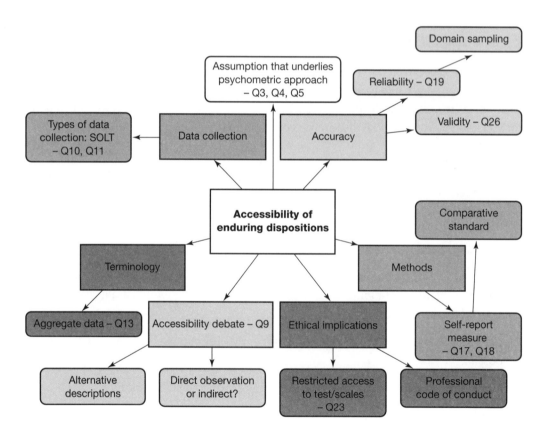

Chapter 2
Personality: evolutionary, physiological and trait approaches

This chapter provides questions relating to the ways in which psychologists have attempted to describe and explain personality, with a particular focus on biological approaches. Topics include the way physiological process can be linked to traits, differences between biological theories, and the impact biological theories have had on *whole-person* personality research.

Select one of the possible answers for each question.

Foundation level questions

1. Which of the following groups includes three key biological approaches to personality?

   A. Behavioural genetics, evolutionary theory and neurophysiology.

   B. Evolutionary theory, behavioural anatomy and neurophysiology.

   C. Evolutionary theory, neurophysiology and chemico-behaviourism.

   D. Behavioural genetics, neuroanatomy and pharmacology.

   Your answer: ☐

2. Which of the following groups includes psychologists who illustrate the biological approach to personality through their work?

   A. Ainsworth (1957), Bowlby (1957) and Freud (1923).

   B. Marx (1848), Rogers (1954) and Weber (1890).

   C. Durkheim (1893), Fish (1926) and Gramsci (1947).

   D. Eysenck (1967), Gray (1970) and Pavlov (1927).

   Your answer: ☐

3. How does Eysenck (1967) attempt to explain personality?

    A. In terms of genetic processes.

    B. In terms of evolutionary concepts.

    C. In terms of neurophysiological processes.

    D. In terms of social processes.

Your answer: ☐

4. Which trait is the ascending reticular activating system linked to?

    A. Neuroticism.

    B. Psychoticism.

    C. Agreeableness.

    D. Extraversion.

Your answer: ☐

5. Observed primary traits and habitual acts are said to reflect what?

    A. An individual's attempts to stimulate their cortical arousal.

    B. An individual's attempts to restore balance in their cortical activity.

    C. An individual's reaction to a situation.

    D. An individual's attempts to unbalance their cortical activity.

Your answer: ☐

6. From the following, what would Eysenck's (1967, 1990) theory expect to find?

    A. Neuroticism being related to physiological measures of emotion.

    B. Neuroticism being related to physiological measures of stimulation.

    C. Extraversion being related to physiological measures of emotion.

    D. Extraversion being related to physiological measures of stimulation.

Your answer: ☐

7. From the following, what would Gray's (1970, 1987, 1990) theory expect to find?

    A. Anxiety is related with high sensitivity to signals of punishment.

    B. Anxiety is associated with low sensitivity to signals of punishment.

    C. Impulsivity is associated with high sensitivity to signals of punishment.

    D. Impulsivity is associated with low sensitivity to signals of reward.

Your answer: ☐

Advanced level questions

8. Which two sets of measures have been used to assess aspects of Eysenck's and Gray's theories?

    A. Measures of the muscular and skeletal system.

    B. Measures of the central nervous system and autonomic nervous system.

    C. Measures of the digestive system and urinary tract.

    D. Measures of the respiratory system and circulatory system.

Your answer: ☐

9. According to Mathews and Gilliland (1999), why are Eysenck's and Gray's theories limited?

    A. Because they are biological theories and not cognitive theories.

    B. Because Mathews and Gilliland do not like Eysenck and Gray.

    C. The relationship between personality traits and EEG and ERP measures are often weak.

    D. None of the above.

Your answer: ☐

10. Broadly, what is the lexical hypothesis?

    A. The attempt of trying to remember a word but being unable to 'access' it.

    B. An assertion that people are distinguishable from one another through natural language.

    C. An assertion that people cannot recognise particular words.

    D. A 'best guess' for language interpretation.

Your answer: ☐

11. What assumption underlies the lexical hypothesis?

A. There exists a finite amount of characteristics or dispositions that describe human variation.

B. There are an infinite number of characteristics that describe human variation.

C. Language is special and must be used in trait psychology.

D. None of the above.

Your answer: ☐

12. What is a key claim about trait adjectives?

A. They are interdependent.

B. They describe real behaviour.

C. They are independent.

D. They are chosen at random.

Your answer: ☐

13. In terms of research, where were the Five Factor traits developed from?

A. Cattell's (1943) use of dimensions to organise traits.

B. Costa and McCrae's (1985) development of an inventory.

C. Goldberg's (1981) description of the five factor traits as the Big Five.

D. A re-analysis of the trait adjectives found in Fiske's (1949) data.

Your answer: ☐

14. How are the Five Factor traits measured?

A. Through adjective and questionnaire statement methods.

B. Through GSR measurements.

C. Through fMRI measurements.

D. Through interviews.

Your answer: ☐

15. Which of the following is the inverse (or bidirectional opposite) of one of the Five Factor traits (FFT)?

   A. Conscientiousness.

   B. Agreeableness.

   C. Emotional stability.

   D. Openness.

Your answer: ☐

16. Which of the following is a key contribution the FFT approach has provided?

   A. A way to develop a standardised measure of traits.

   B. The development of a random measure of personality.

   C. A small number of traits to analyse behaviour.

   D. A larger number of traits to analyse behaviour.

Your answer: ☐

17. What is a disadvantage of the method-sensitive nature of the FFT approach?

   A. It questions the reliability of the FFT.

   B. It questions the conceptual robustness of the FFT.

   C. It questions the measurement of the FFT.

   D. It highlights questions of how research is conducted with the FFT.

Your answer: ☐

18. Which of the following is an objection to the trait approach?

   A. Focuses heavily upon personality function.

   B. Not enough focus on the experimental methods that can be employed.

   C. Focuses heavily upon personality structure.

   D. Not enough focus on correlational designs.

Your answer: ☐

19.   What does the person-situation debate refer to?

A. People that find situations difficult.

B. The stability of personality traits across situations.

C. The stability of people's behaviour across situations.

D. The stability of situations across people.

Your answer:

20. How is an integrative approach to personality likely to shape the discipline?

A. Focus more heavily upon environmental frameworks.

B. Broaden methodological scope to focus on the causes of personality.

C. Detract from traits per se, onto a more reflexive account of personality.

D. None of the above.

Your answer:

21. In terms of evolution which of the following is *not* a process of change?

A. Genetic drift.

B. Natural selection.

C. Mutation.

D. Conservation.

Your answer:

22. What are the predictions of Eysenck's hierarchical model of personality?

A. Super trait → narrow trait → habitual act.

B. Super trait → trait → habitual act.

C. Super trait → intermediate trait → habitual act.

D. Super trait → narrow trait → deviant behaviour.

Your answer:

Extended multiple-choice question

Complete the following paragraph using the items listed below. Not all items can be used because not all items will be consistent with the paragraph. Items can only be used once.

There is a wealth of evidence that supports the Five _____ Model of personality. For example, the factor constructs have been _____ identified in various cultures and languages through self and peer reports (Caprara and Cervone, 2000); the biological indicators of some of the traits, that is the _____ between scores on personality inventories, have shown physiological _____ between individuals. There remains apprehension in concluding that these factors will have an _____ role in a _____ theory of personality (ibid.). This is partly because of the kinds of studies the FFM produces which often identify and describe how two things _____, for example, the variance of a student's conscientiousness score and the _____ this has with their mathematics exam score. Thus there is no _____ link that is explained in this research. Therefore, while the FFM describes the structure of personality, there remains space for a functional integrative theory to better understand and _____ personality.

Optional items

A. Factor

B. association

C. reliably

D. variability

E. differences

F. similarities

G. co-occur

H. correlation

I. mixed

J. causal

K. explain

L. describe

M. enduring

N. scientific

Essay questions for Chapter 2

Once you have completed the MCQs above you should be ready to tackle some essay questions. You might like to select three or four topics and make notes on them. One way to do this is to create a concept map. The concept map for the first question has been done for you and you can see how the knowledge required links to some of the MCQs in this chapter.

1. Compare and contrast Eysenck's (1967, 1990) and Gray's (1970, 1987, 1990) physiological approaches to personality.

2. How useful is evolutionary theory for explaining human variation? What does the theory have problems explaining? Discuss.

3. Critically consider how Eysenck's theory of personality (Eysenck et al., 1992) crosses over both biological and trait approaches. How do neurophysiological processes attempt to explain personality?

4. To what extent might an integrative approach extend the direction of research on personality?

5. How has the psychometric approach shaped the way personality has been conceptualised and researched? Explain and illustrate with examples.

6. To what extent is the Five Factor Model a comprehensive account of personality?

7. Critically evaluate the claim that 'personality can predict behaviour'.

8. In what ways do trait measures differ from physiological measures of personality? Are there any areas of agreement between them?

Chapter 2 essay question 1: concept map

Compare and contrast Eysenck's (1967, 1990) and Gray's (1970, 1987, 1990) physiological approaches to personality.

The concept map below provides an example of the topic areas that you might include when writing your essay. Remember that it is important to link your answers to other topic areas not covered in this chapter. You might consider each theory in terms of the biological approach to personality and then discuss the distinctive features that make the theories different. You might also consider how both theories fit with the whole-person approach to personality before you draw a final conclusion.

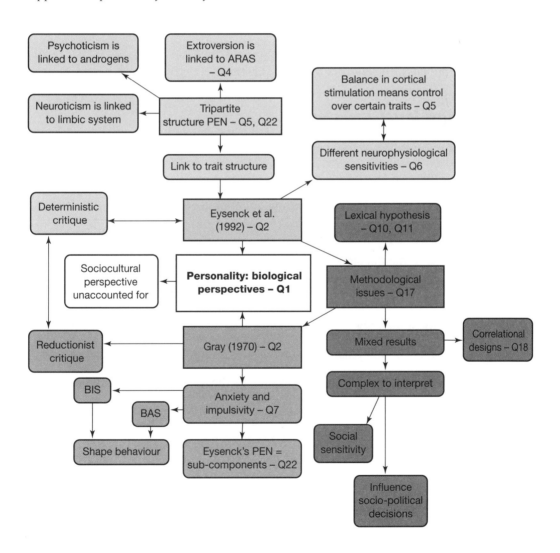

Chapter 3
Genetics and environment: a view of individuality and uniqueness

This chapter provides questions relating to the ways in which psychologists have attempted to link personality and individual differences to genetic and environmental factors. Topics include the aims and methods of genetic and environmental interpretations of personality as well as how the integration of genetic and environmental factors are taking personality theory and research forward.

Select one of the possible answers for each question.

Foundation level questions

1. In terms of personality, why is it important to account for differences in genes?

    A. To map a gene history for individuals.

    B. To better understand how the environment affects personality.

    C. To find out what people are like.

    D. To find environmental similarities.

    Your answer:

2. In reference to personality, what is a psychological construct?

    A. A mental concept that leads to self-awareness via the mind–body interaction.

    B. A mental concept that remembers events via the mind–body interaction.

    C. A mental concept that influences behaviour via the mind–body interaction.

    D. A mental concept that supresses behaviour via the mind–body interaction.

    Your answer:

3. What is a key aim of behavioural genetic research?

   A. To unpack numerically 'elements' of personality attributable to genetic and environmental influence.

   B. To find differences from one individual to another within a population or group of people.

   C. To anger developmental psychologists.

   D. To make personality sound more complex than it might be.

Your answer: ☐

4. Gottesman (1963) advocated which approach to the 'nature-nurture debate'?

   A. A determinist approach.

   B. An interaction approach.

   C. A reductionist approach.

   D. An essentialist approach.

Your answer: ☐

5. Which of the following is an example of the *reaction range*?

   A. People react to a reward stimulus.

   B. An individual's height is solely determined by environmental factors.

   C. An individual's height is solely determined by inherited factors.

   D. Potential height is inherited, but actual height is made likely by environmental factors such as your diet.

Your answer: ☐

6. In terms of genetics what does the phenotype refer to?

   A. Observable characteristics of an individual.

   B. Inherited genetic make-up of an individual.

   C. Solely environmental factors.

   D. A condition that makes people act in a feline manner.

Your answer: ☐

7. Which of the following best describes what environment means as a generic term?

A. The physical world.

B. The social world.

C. All influences other than inherited factors.

D. All influences that only include genetic factors.

Your answer: ☐

8. What genetic feature enables observation of environmental influences on an individual's genotype?

A. Heritability.

B. Mitosis.

C. The reciprocal relationship between DNA and RNA.

D. Meiosis.

Your answer: ☐

9. Which of the following is part of the basic premise of behavioural genetic research?

A. Error variance.

B. Epigenetic variance.

C. Nurture variance.

D. Other variance.

Your answer: ☐

10. Which from the following does *observable variance* tend to refer to in genetic behavioural research?

A. Only environmental variation.

B. Only genetic variation.

C. Statistical variation.

D. None of the above.

Your answer: ☐

Advanced level questions

11. What is one way behavioural geneticists investigate whether or not personality is inherited?

    A. Through twin studies.

    B. Through single-child studies.

    C. Through studying DNA.

    D. Through single-parent studies.

Your answer: ☐

12. Once behavioural genetic variance and 'shared environmental' variance have been accounted for what is left?

    A. Genetic variance.

    B. Unexplained variance.

    C. Lost variance.

    D. Hidden variance.

Your answer: ☐

13. Which of the following is one objection to behavioural genetic methods?

    A. The 'non-equal environments assumption'.

    B. The 'stimulus environment assumption'.

    C. The 'dehumanisation environment assumption'.

    D. The 'equal environments assumption'.

Your answer: ☐

14. Which of the following stems from many genes that vary in activity depending on environmental context?

    A. Cystic fibrosis.

    B. Huntington's disease.

    C. Early onset Alzheimer's.

    D. Weight.

Your answer: ☐

15. How is a psychological definition of personality different from a lay definition?

    A. Psychological definitions predict behaviour; lay definitions do not.

    B. Psychological definitions categorise people; lay definitions do not.

    C. Lay definitions are based on fiction whereas psychological definitions are based on fact.

    D. Psychological definitions operationalise personality in terms of characteristics or qualities typical to an individual.

Your answer: ☐

16. What does intra-individual variation refer to?

    A. Interaction between two individuals.

    B. Variation of interaction between the individual and situation.

    C. Interaction between situations.

    D. Non-interaction.

Your answer: ☐

17. What does inter-individual variation refer to?

    A. Similarities and differences between persons.

    B. Similarities and differences between groups.

    C. Similarities between persons.

    D. Differences between persons.

Your answer: ☐

18. Which theory is asserted when describing someone as having 'no personality'?

    A. Explicit personality theory.

    B. Lay personality theory.

    C. Implicit personality theory.

    D. Quadruplicity personality theory.

Your answer: ☐

19. What does research suggest is the best predictor for changes in personality scores?

    A. Genetic factors in early adulthood.

    B. Genetic factors in early and middle adulthood.

    C. Environmental factors in childhood.

    D. Environmental factors in both early and middle adulthood.

Your answer: ☐

20. Which of the following is one environmental measure that accounts for influences on personality?

    A. QTL methods.

    B. Galvanic skin response methods.

    C. fMRI scans.

    D. Identical (i.e. monozygotic) twins who are reared in different families.

Your answer: ☐

21. Evidence indicates what aspects of the Five Factors to be heritable?

    A. Self-monitoring aspects.

    B. Group-monitoring aspects.

    C. Peer-monitoring aspects.

    D. Job-monitoring aspects.

Your answer: ☐

22. Penke et al. (2007) suggest which of the following is best at explaining genetic variance in personality traits?

    A. Selective neutrality.

    B. Mutation-selection balance.

    C. Balancing selection by environmental heterogeneity.

    D. Selective conservation.

Your answer: ☐

Extended multiple-choice question 1

Complete Figure 3.1 using the items listed below. Not all items can be used because not all items will be the bidirectional opposite of each of the five factor super-categories. Items can only be used once.

Figure 3.1 Costa and McCrae's (1992) Five Factor Traits (FFT)

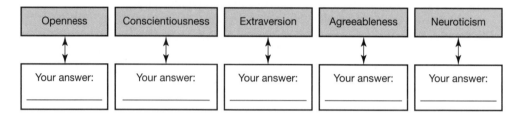

Optional items

A. closedness to experience

B. psychoticism

C. lack of direction

D. dutifulness

E. introversion

F. positive emotions

G. antagonism

H. compliance

I. emotional stability

J. gregariousness

Extended multiple-choice question 2

Match the 'lower-order' factors that go with each 'higher-order' factor (i.e. openness, extraversion and agreeableness) in Figure 3.2 from the items listed below. Not all the items can be used because some do not belong to the 'higher-order' factors presented. Choose three 'lower order' factors for each 'higher order' factor.

Figure 3.2 Three of Costa and McCrae's (1992) higher-order traits and six facets

Openness	Extraversion	Agreeableness

- _____
- _____
- _____

- _____
- _____
- _____

- _____
- _____
- _____

Optional items

A. assertiveness

B. ideas

C. actions

D. aesthetics

E. impulsiveness

F. warmth

G. deliberation

H. activity

I. trust

J. anxiety

K. modesty

L. depression

M. achievement striving

N. altruism

Essay questions for Chapter 3

Once you have completed the MCQs above you should be ready to tackle some essay questions. You might like to select three or four topics and make notes on them. One way to do this is to create a concept map. The concept map for the first question has been done for you and you can see how the knowledge required links to some of the MCQs in this chapter.

1. How useful are behavioural genetic approaches for explaining human variation? What do they have problems with explaining? Discuss.

2. Discuss the difficulties associated with defining personality.

3. How has the genetic approach contributed to our understanding of personality? Explain and illustrate with examples.

4. Examine critically evidence that suggests specific collections of genes might be linked to certain aspects of personality. What are the major implications of this research? Discuss.

5. Evaluate the Five Factor Traits in comparison to the PEN model of personality.

6. To what extent is the person-situation debate relevant to contemporary personality research?

7. In what ways do structuralism approaches differ from functionalism approaches to personality interpretation in their aims and methods? Are there any areas of agreement between them?

8. Examine critically the relevance of an integrative approach to personality.

9. Critically assess whether personality research traces numerically sources of variance or causes.

10. Discuss how behavioural genetic research has contributed to understanding environmental contributions to personality.

Chapter 3 essay question 1: concept map

How useful are behavioural genetic approaches for explaining human variation? What do they have problems explaining? Discuss.

The concept map below provides an example of the topic areas that you might include when writing your essay. Consideration of behaviour genetics to human individuality and uniqueness leads to several sub-topics. You may choose to describe and evaluate some sub-topics before you draw conclusions based on the majority of the evidence presented. Remember that it is important to link your answers to other topic areas not covered in this chapter.

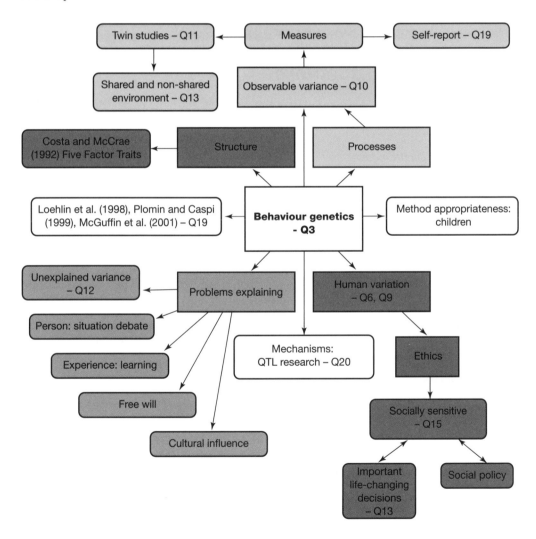

Chapter 4
Personality: a reflection on physical health

This chapter provides questions relating to how physical health and disease have been linked to personality and individual differences. Topics include aims and methods relating to personality types, conceptual and methodological issues and contemporary developments.

Select one of the possible answers for each question.

Foundation level questions

1. What is a key category associated with the biomedical model of health?

   A. Absence of disease.

   B. Occurrence of disease.

   C. Absence of illness.

   D. Absence of any stimulus.

   Your answer:

2. Which of the following is one objection to the biomedical model?

   A. Its association with illness.

   B. A lack of focus on psychosocial factors essential to the diagnostic process.

   C. The non-medical focus.

   D. Does not account for biological evidence on health.

   Your answer:

3. What does TABP stand for?

   A. Transverse analytic behavioural pattern.

   B. Technical aggregate behavioural pattern.

   C. Type A behavioural proneness.

   D. Type A behaviour pattern.

   Your answer:

4. Which of the following is a description of TABP?

   A. Traits that are provoked by environmental factors.

   B. Traits that are provoked by genetic factors.

   C. Specific behavioural reaction styles provoked by environmental cues.

   D. Specific behavioural reaction styles provoked by genetic cues.

Your answer: ☐

5. Which of the following is one measure of Type A and B behaviour patterns?

   A. Jenkins Activity Survey.

   B. fMRI scans.

   C. GSR.

   D. Rorschach inkblot tests.

Your answer: ☐

6. Which of the following describes Type C personality?

   A. A Cartesian personality factor.

   B. The traits associated with cravings.

   C. People that lack cortical arousal.

   D. Psychosocial risk factor for the development of cancer.

Your answer: ☐

7. What does the Grossarth-Maticek typology refer to?

   A. Six behavioural reaction styles.

   B. Types of behavioural stimulants.

   C. A way to encourage habit forming.

   D. Types of personality traits.

Your answer: ☐

Advanced level questions

8. Which biomedical heuristic is used to describe physical and psychological deviations from the 'norm'?

A. Conformation bias.

B. Representativeness.

C. Normative standard.

D. Horn's effect.

Your answer: ☐

9. Broadly, what is the biopsychosocial model of health?

A. A personality trait.

B. The name of a famous behavioural scientist.

C. A framework to conceptualise physical and psychological health.

D. A model that relates to the causes of stress.

Your answer: ☐

10. Which of the following is a biopsychosocial model?

A. The treatment model.

B. The diathesis-stress model.

C. The psychosomatic model.

D. Fisher's (1929) model.

Your answer: ☐

11. Which of the following is a critique of the biopsychosocial model?

A. Focus on power imbalance.

B. Focus on status imbalance.

C. Focus on psychodynamics.

D. Limited biomedical interpretations.

Your answer: ☐

12. Which option emphasises a more contemporary aspect of the biopsychosocial model?

A. Emotions.

B. Artificial intelligence.

C. Emphasis on pseudoscientific evidence.

D. Statistics.

Your answer: ☐

13. How have personality and physical health been linked?

A. By the identification of disease.

B. Through the Internet evidence base.

C. Through personality processes that function as self-regulation.

D. Through plausible behaviour reactions.

Your answer: ☐

14. What was one aim of Friedman and Roseman's (1957, 1959) work?

A. To provide an alternative framework to personality.

B. To account for the rise in rates of cardiovascular morbidity and mortality.

C. To identify non-specific behaviours.

D. To be scientific.

Your answer: ☐

15. Evidence indicates which TABP measure to more accurately predict cardiovascular disease?

A. Structured interview.

B. Jenkins Activity Survey.

C. NEO-PI-R.

D. EPI.

Your answer: ☐

16. What typical characteristics are associated with Type C personality?

    A. High levels of extraversion, low levels of neuroticism.

    B. Low levels of neuroticism, high levels of extraversion.

    C. Agreeableness.

    D. Conscientiousness.

Your answer: ☐

17. Neuroticism has been found to predict which of the following?

    A. Risk of developing cancer.

    B. Cancer survival.

    C. Cancer acceptance.

    D. Cancer decline.

Your answer: ☐

18. What does Type C research on behavioural reaction styles suggest?

    A. Type C people are unfortunate.

    B. Type C personality predicts disease.

    C. Certain behavioural reaction styles are possibly more disease prone.

    D. People should not react.

Your answer: ☐

19. According to Amelang (1997) what is a flaw to the six typology of personality?

    A. Personality types are not independent.

    B. Personality types are independent.

    C. There are in fact more types.

    D. There are in fact fewer types.

Your answer: ☐

20. Disease-prone personality research has produced which results?

  A. Curvilinear.

  B. Linear.

  C. Negative.

  D. Mixed.

Your answer: ☐

21. According to Gallo and Matthews (2003) socio-economic status relates to emotional and cognitive symptoms that on evaluation can predict what?

  A. Worse health outcomes.

  B. Better health.

  C. Burdensome health.

  D. Long-term health.

Your answer: ☐

22. What has research demonstrated in the link between personality traits and self-rated health measures?

  A. Traits are stable.

  B. Traits are non-existent.

  C. Traits are related more closely to self-rated physical health rather than actual physical health.

  D. Traits are related to actual physical health.

Your answer: ☐

23. Which of the following are characteristics of Type D personality?

  A. Low levels of negative affect and social inhibition.

  B. High levels of negative affect and social inhibition.

  C. High levels of agreeableness.

  D. Low levels of agreeableness.

Your answer: ☐

24. Which one of the following was Type D personality specifically developed to predict?

    A. Clinical outcomes (e.g. response to surgery).

    B. Survival factors.

    C. Risk factors.

    D. All-cause mortality.

Your answer: ☐

Extended multiple-choice question

Complete the following paragraph using the items listed below and opposite. Not all items can be used because not all items will be consistent with the paragraph. Items can only be used once.

There has been a lengthy precedence of the link between personality, _____ _____ and disease processes. A key premise is that _____ factors are implicated with individual differences in the recovery and possibly the _____ of physical health or disease. For example, Friedman and Rosenman (1959) were able to relate processes of cardiovascular disease with certain behaviour patterns in middle-aged men; this link has been described as Type _____ behaviour pattern (TABP) with _____ behaviours described as Type _____ behaviour pattern. However, the link between TABP and cardiovascular disease has been questioned on the grounds of _____ dependency. Nevertheless, there is compelling evidence that TABP can predict the likely onset of _____ disease (Lachar, 1993). An important focus to come from this research is the link between _____ and behaviour that mediates personality and physical health (ibid.).

Optional items

A. physical health

B. mental health

C. psychological

D. physiological

E. onset

F. C

G. A

H. B

I. method

J. cardiovascular

K. emotion

L. opposite

Essay questions for Chapter 4

Once you have completed the MCQs above you should be ready to tackle some essay questions. You might like to select three or four topics and make notes on them. One way to do this is to create a concept map. The concept map for the first question has been done for you and you can see how the knowledge required links to some of the MCQs in this chapter.

1. Critically evaluate the definition of health as being free from disease.

2. Why can the whole-person approach to the personality link to health not be understood unless it is set in a biopsychosocial context? Discuss.

3. Critically discuss what is meant by disease-prone personality in terms of evidence from Type A and B behaviour pattern.

4. Compare and contrast conceptual and methodological issues related to Type A and Type C personality.

5. Compare and contrast conceptual and research evidence of the Grossarth-Maticek typology to the classification of persons into personality types.

6. Identify critically features of Type D personality and what the research on the identified features *actually* demonstrates.

7. How are personality traits linked to physical health and well-being? Explain and illustrate with examples.

8. Examine critically the claim that 'personality can be linked to a specific disease'.

Chapter 4 essay question 1: concept map

Critically evaluate the definition of health as being free from disease.

The concept map below provides an example of how the first sample essay might be conceptualised. Consideration of the whole-person approach to individual differences psychology leads to two main approaches that overarch several sub-topics you can critically evaluate before you draw any conclusions.

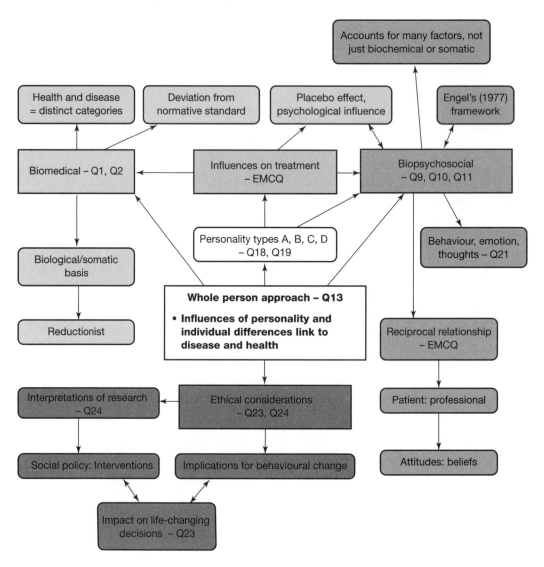

Chapter 5
Intelligence and individual differences

This chapter provides questions relating to intelligence and individual differences. Topics include why intelligence is important, the central contention of definitions of intelligence, approaches, measures and methods of intelligence, and what the evidence *actually* demonstrates.

Select one of the possible answers for each question.

Foundation level questions

1. Which of the following is not a word that might be used to describe people's ideas of intelligence?

    A. Perceive.

    B. Evaluate.

    C. Decisions.

    D. Relinquish.

    Your answer: ☐

2. In what way might perception of intelligence improve likely employment?

    A. A candidate perceived as intelligent will be more likely to get the job.

    B. A candidate perceived as unintelligent will be more likely to get the job.

    C. A candidate perceived as intelligent is less likely to get the job.

    D. A candidate perceived as unintelligent is less likely to get the job.

    Your answer: ☐

3. How might ideas of what intelligence is allow parents to shape their decisions about their children?

    A. It would allow parents to know when to correct their child/children if they make an error.

    B. It would allow parents to justify when they shout at their child/children.

    C. It would allow parents to emotionally blackmail their children.

    D. It could help improve parents' love for their child/children.

Your answer: ☐

4. Which of the following is one practical application for intelligence data?

    A. To fill time.

    B. To give statisticians something to do.

    C. In the assessment of armed service recruits in terms of 'job' allocation.

    D. To give third parties the opportunity to use this data.

Your answer: ☐

5. What was Galton's (1865) central hypothesis on intelligence?

    A. There are differences in intelligence.

    B. Animals are all the same in terms of intelligence.

    C. Intelligence is too complex to measure.

    D. He was the most intelligent person of his time.

Your answer: ☐

6. Which of the following is one of Binet's (1905) lasting contributions to intelligence testing?

    A. Matching a child's eye colour with their test score.

    B. Matching 'mental age' with test score.

    C. Matching an animal with a child's test score.

    D. Matching test score with the number of behaviour problems a child has.

Your answer: ☐

7. How do measures of intelligence differ from personality trait measures?

   A. Intelligence = knowledge; personality traits = behaviour.

   B. Intelligence = mind; personality traits = body.

   C. Intelligence = common sense; personality traits = lack of common sense.

   D. Intelligence = correlation between test scores; personality traits = correlations to responses between individual items.

   Your answer: ☐

Advanced level questions

8. Which of the following is one important way the Wechsler tests departed from previous intelligence tests?

   A. They measure adult phobia, previous tests did not.

   B. Wechsler scales were designed so all people of all ages could take them.

   C. They measure eye colour correlation with test score.

   D. They measure only what young people *can do*.

   Your answer: ☐

9. What is missing from William Stern's (1912) definition of intelligence shown below?
   (_____ ÷ chronological age × 100) = IQ

   A. IQ.

   B. Chronological age.

   C. Mental age.

   D. Number of people in the sample.

   Your answer: ☐

10. Which of the following psychologists is associated with the information processing approach to intellect?

    A. Spearman (1904).

    B. Sternberg (1988).

    C. Warden (1951).

    D. Slater (1981).

    Your answer: ☐

11. What according to Spearman (1904) do the *g* factor and *s* factor stand for?

    A. Gross mathematic ability and structured ability.

    B. Grand capacity and slow capacity.

    C. General mental ability and specific factors.

    D. Glowing ability and submerged factors.

Your answer: ☐

12. How do the learning approaches contrast with other approaches to intelligence?

    A. Focus on behaviour rather than mental activity.

    B. Focus on mental activity rather than behaviour.

    C. Focus on knowledge rather than experience.

    D. None of the above.

Your answer: ☐

13. Which of the following is *not* a problem identified by Neisworth and Bagnato (2004) with the use of standardised psychological tests?

    A. Testing is detrimental.

    B. Authentic assessment is superior.

    C. True functioning is assessed.

    D. Based on convention not evidence.

Your answer: ☐

14. How do psychometricians operationally define intelligence?

    A. By using children in their data collection.

    B. By using adults in their data collection.

    C. By using domain sampling.

    D. By using a representative sample.

Your answer: ☐

15. Zigler et al. (1973) found *motivation* to do what for 'lower' -class children's desire to do well on IQ tests?

   A. Decreased their test performance by 10 IQ points.

   B. Nothing.

   C. Improved their test performance by 10 IQ points.

   D. Improved their perception of IQ tests.

Your answer: ☐

16. What is one objection to explicit standardised tests of intellectual ability?

   A. Domain sampling.

   B. Range restriction.

   C. Limited validity.

   D. Limited accuracy.

Your answer: ☐

17. Dove (1968) developed the Dove Counterbalance General Intelligence Test for what main reason?

   A. To counteract culture bias in intelligence testing.

   B. To test people's knowledge.

   C. To test people's behaviour.

   D. To test other psychologists.

Your answer: ☐

18. What is a key disadvantage to evidence on race and biological links with intelligence?

   A. We might discover women are better than men at all tasks.

   B. Such research raises important ethical issues and is socially sensitive.

   C. We might find unbelievable answers.

   D. We might find there is no relationship with these factors.

Your answer: ☐

19. Brown (1992) advocates intellectual ability is best understood where?

    A. Within statistical analysis.

    B. Within the neuroanatomy of groups of people.

    C. Within the biological differences of individuals.

    D. Within the context in which it happens.

Your answer: ☐

20. Which from the following is an essential criterion for psychologists?

    A. Writing as many academic papers as possible.

    B. Finding participants for other people's research.

    C. Writing controversial academic papers.

    D. To account for the ethical and political decisions that are implicated with explicit standardised mental ability tests.

Your answer: ☐

21. What is a feature that older definitions of intelligence share with more contemporary definitions?

    A. The conceptualisation that intelligence is essential for self-regulation.

    B. Brain size matters.

    C. Finding individuals with inferior intellect.

    D. Brain size does not matter.

Your answer: ☐

22. Why is it difficult to find a universally accepted definition of intelligence?

    A. Because people do not care.

    B. Because definitions are surrounded by past, present and possibly future debates of the construct (intelligence).

    C. Because psychologists purposefully disagree with each other.

    D. Because there is no indirect way to actually measure intelligence.

Your answer: ☐

23. Which of the following is not part of Sternberg's (1988) triarchic theory?

   A. Componential.

   B. Contextual.

   C. Experiential.

   D. Exponential.

Your answer: ☐

24. Which of the following is not a model used to describe the different theoretical approaches to intelligence?

   A. Lumpers.

   B. Splitters.

   C. Eclectic.

   D. Hierarchical.

Your answer: ☐

25. A fundamental premise of Spearman's (1904) theory was that the _____ of intelligence could be identified through statistical methods. Two of the most popular choices are the _____ method and _____ .

   A. Processes, experimental, factor analysis.

   B. Causal mechanisms, experimental, correlational.

   C. Structure, correlational, factor analysis.

   D. Association, experimental, meta-analytic.

Your answer: ☐

26. Which of the following appear to underpin measured cognitive intelligence?

   A. Working memory and processing speed.

   B. Long-term memory and lexical access.

   C. Short-term memory and processing speed.

   D. Average memory and language processes.

Your answer: ☐

27. Which of the following is an important point that can be drawn from the work of Deary et al. (2010)?

A. The relationship between genotype and phenotype is simple.

B. The relationship between genotype and phenotype is complex and must not be oversimplified.

C. Biological determinants of intelligence are only genetically based.

D. Biological determinants of intelligence say nothing about cognitive ability.

Your answer: ☐

28. Which of the following is an important point about approaches that claim social factors determine intelligence?

A. Many of these approaches are not exclusively social as they often use a biopsychosocial framework.

B. Many of these approaches do not account for social factors of intelligence.

C. Intelligence is biologically determined and social approaches find it difficult to interpret intelligence for this reason.

D. Social approaches are less diverse than biological approaches that claim intelligence is determined by these separate factors.

Your answer: ☐

Extended multiple-choice question

Complete the following paragraph using the items listed opposite. Not all items can be used because not all items will be consistent with the paragraph. Items can only be used once.

The use and _____ of intellectual ability tests by academics and non-academics have far-reaching _____ for people. For example, a controversy was unleashed when the possible link between race and IQ was made by Jensen (1969), who suggested black people have innately lower IQs because on average their scores were lower than whites on the same standardised intellectual ability test. However, this research is flawed from a genetic perspective as we cannot suggest there is more genetic _____ in one racial group than _____ racial groups. Therefore socio-political _____ are of central relevance in the prevention of potential or _____ misrepresented use and interpretation of explicit _____ tests.

Optional items

A. interpretation

B. problems

C. consequences

D. intelligence

E. variation

F. significance

G. between

H. implications

I. actual

J. standardised

Essay questions for Chapter 5

Once you have completed the MCQs above you should be ready to tackle some essay questions. You might like to select three or four topics and make notes on them. One way to do this is to create a concept map. The concept map for the first question has been done for you and you can see how the knowledge required links to some of the MCQs in this chapter.

1. Critically evaluate Gardner's (1983, 1995) multiple intelligences theory. What are the implications for the 'unique cognitive profile' approach?

2. Compare and contrast two information processing approaches to intelligence.

3. Intelligence tests allow psychologists to identify individuals with *inferior intellect*. Critically discuss this statement, explain and illustrate with relevant examples.

4. Critically evaluate Spearman's (1904) *general intelligence factor* with Sternberg's (2005) *componential* approach to intelligence.

5. Discuss the implications of the psychometric approach to intelligence research.

6. In what way is Spearman's (1904) approach to intelligence different from Thurstone's (1938) approach? Are there any areas of agreement between them?

7. Critically evaluate how intelligent behaviour has been defined with reference to Sternberg's (2005) work.

8. In what way do biological approaches differ from social approaches to 'our' understanding of human intelligence? Are there any areas of agreement between them?

Chapter 5 essay question 1: concept map

Critically evaluate Gardner's (1983, 1995) multiple intelligences theory. What are the implications for the 'unique cognitive profile' approach?

The concept map below provides an example of how the first sample essay might be conceptualised. Consideration of evidence in support of and evidence that contradicts Gardner's (1983, 1995) theory is necessary before a sound conclusion can be made. You might also consider life domain examples such as how this theory could be/has been applied to educational settings. Remember that it is important to link your answers to other topic areas not covered in this chapter.

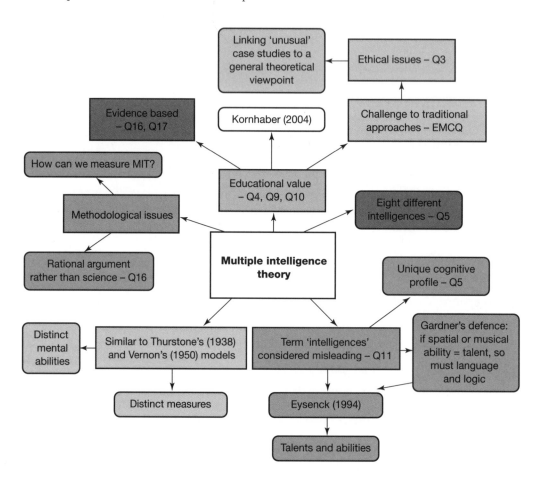

Chapter 6
Personality development across the lifespan

This chapter provides questions relating to personality development across the lifespan. It includes topics such as possible changes in personality structure from childhood to adulthood, patterns for the change and continuity of personality, principles that can influence change and continuity, and what the research *actually* demonstrates.

Select one of the possible answers for each question.

Foundation level questions

1. How do temperament traits differ from personality traits?

    A. Temperament traits appear later and are considered higher-level traits.

    B. Temperament traits predict animal behaviour.

    C. Temperament traits appear earlier and are considered lower-level traits.

    D. Temperament traits are for small children only.

Your answer: ☐

2. What is one similarity both temperament traits and personality traits share?

    A. Experiences are shaped by environmental factors.

    B. They are temper bound.

    C. Psychologists do not think either is important for the individual.

    D. Both are observable in non-human species.

Your answer: ☐

3. Which of the following describes what is meant by taxonomy of traits?

   A. The identification of causes of personality.

   B. The identification of affects of personality.

   C. The identification of a reliable pattern of covariation of traits across individuals.

   D. A personality trait that is taxing on the individual.

Your answer: ☐

4. Which factor allows children to display an increasingly differentiated set of traits?

   A. Saturation.

   B. Maturation.

   C. Gregariousness.

   D. Modularisation.

Your answer: ☐

5. Children's temperament traits are often considered in light of which aspect?

   A. Their emotion.

   B. Their intelligence.

   C. Their gender.

   D. Their culture.

Your answer: ☐

6. What is one type of data that can be used to identify individual differences over long stretches of the lifespan?

   A. Short-term data.

   B. Intermediate data.

   C. Advanced data.

   D. Longitudinal data.

Your answer: ☐

7. Which from the following is not associated with increasing personality consistency with age?

    A. Niche building.

    B. The process of developing, committing to and maintaining an identity.

    C. Normative developmental changes.

    D. Non-normative developmental changes.

    Your answer: ☐

Advanced level questions

8. What does rank-order stability reflect?

    A. Test-retest summed score.

    B. Cumulative score differentials.

    C. Comparison of ANOVA and MANOVA data outputs.

    D. Test-retest correlations.

    Your answer: ☐

9. Which of the options would be predicted by the radical contextual perspective to personality?

    A. Personality is prone to change but will yield high test-retest correlation coefficients.

    B. Personality is static and only changes under major environmental factors.

    C. Personality is fluid, prone to change and likely to yield low test-retest correlation coefficients.

    D. Personality is biologically based and not susceptible to influences of the environment.

    Your answer: ☐

10. What has evidence suggested about rank-order stability?

   A. Personality traits are only modestly susceptible to change after the age of 50.

   B. Personality traits change massively after the age of 50.

   C. Personality traits do not change one little bit after the age of 50.

   D. People do not have personality after the age of 50.

Your answer: ☐

11. Which of the following refers to mean level change in personality development?

   A. Changes in the average weight of a sample within a population.

   B. Variation in the average colour preference.

   C. Changes in the average level of attitude toward personality questionnaires.

   D. Changes in the average trait level of a population.

Your answer: ☐

12. In terms of the Big Five, dominance (subcomponent of extraversion) yields what pattern across the life course?

   A. Traits associated with dominance cannot be found after the age of 4.

   B. Traits associated with dominance cannot be found after 0 years of age.

   C. Traits associated with dominance increased from adolescence through early middle age.

   D. Traits associated with dominance decreased from adolescence through early middle age.

Your answer: ☐

13. What do higher-order personality traits predict among children?

   A. Social incompetence.

   B. Social competence.

   C. Social maladjustment.

   D. Differences to adult personality.

Your answer: ☐

14. What has research shown for children high on negative emotionality or low on constraint?

   A. Children tend to be withdrawn from any activities.

   B. Children tend to be more enthusiastic across time.

   C. Children tend to have a number of social difficulties concurrently and across time.

   D. Children tend to have a number of enhanced social functioning abilities concurrently and across time.

Your answer: ☐

15. According to Karney and Bradbury (1995) which of the following are strong predictors of relationship outcomes?

   A. Neuroticism and agreeableness.

   B. Conscientiousness and agreeableness.

   C. Openness and neuroticism.

   D. Extraversion and neuroticism.

Your answer: ☐

16. According to Shiner (2000) which personality trait predicts academic achievement across time into adulthood?

   A. Agreeableness.

   B. Introversion.

   C. Conscientiousness.

   D. Openness to experience.

Your answer: ☐

17. Why is the finding that personality effects on achievement emerge early in life important?

   A. Because of the cumulative effects that school adjustment and academic performance have over time.

   B. Because of the consequences on social adjustment into old age.

   C. Because of the way it shapes parents' attitudes toward school teachers.

   D. Because of the way it influences teachers' perception of parents.

Your answer: ☐

18. In what way are traits of conscientiousness/constraint important across the life course?

    A. They are non-cognitive predictors of educational achievement.

    B. They are cognitive predictors of educational achievement.

    C. These traits predict a person's favourite subject/topic area in terms of education.

    D. These traits are social predictors of educational achievement.

Your answer: ☐

19. According to Birch and Ladd (1998) children's personalities can potentially influence what?

    A. Their emerging relationships with their teachers.

    B. Their emerging relationships with their friends.

    C. Their emerging relationships with their imaginary friend.

    D. Their relationship with themselves.

Your answer: ☐

20. Hazan and Shaver (1987) discovered a link between early attachment experiences and later adult romantic relationships. This is an example of what?

    A. A modal model of memory.

    B. A working memory model.

    C. The internal working model.

    D. The external working model.

Your answer: ☐

21. Who from the following is not an age-stage theorist?

    A. Loevinger (1966).

    B. Erickson (1963).

    C. Piaget (1896–1980).

    D. Dawkins (2008).

Your answer: ☐

22. Which of the following most aptly characterises the age-stage approach?

    A. The age-stage approach serves as a broad metaphor for partitioning the lifecycle.

    B. Chronological age matches psychological stages through the lifespan.

    C. The age-stage approach is theoretically possible.

    D. The age-stage approach is inadequate in capturing the multifaceted nature of self-control processes.

Your answer: ☐

23. What does the longitudinal research on cognitive development show in terms of the heritability of IQ?

    A. IQ decreases from early childhood through to late adolescence.

    B. IQ remains equal from early childhood through to late adolescence.

    C. IQ increases from early childhood through to late adolescence.

    D. None of the above.

Your answer: ☐

24. What is one key finding from behavioural genetic research?

    A. The 'environment' exists.

    B. Environmental experiences tend to create differences between children growing up in different families.

    C. Genetics does not matter to a child's development of personality.

    D. Genetics does not impact on adult personality.

Your answer: ☐

Extended multiple-choice question

Complete the following paragraph using the items listed below. Not all items can be used because not all items will be consistent with the paragraph. Items can only be used once.

Research on cognitive _____ indicates that IQ heritability estimates _____ from early childhood through to late adolescence (Plomin et al., 1997). Thus the balance of genetic versus _____ influences varies at successive developmental 'stages'. Findings also suggest that 'shared environmental' factors have less _____ on the effect of IQ between siblings as they age which has been attributed to the fact that siblings increasingly seek out environments _____ with their own genetic endowments. However, _____ must be acutely aware of the high-level _____ making that at times accompanies the interpretation of such results which is a key reason for taking a _____ _____ stance toward personality outcomes and lifespan development research (Yanchar et al., 2008).

Optional items

A. development

B. decreases

C. increase

D. environmental

E. influence

F. pronunciation

G. professionals

H. academics

I. decision-making

J. associated

K. correlated

L. critical thinking

M. analytic thinking

Essay questions for Chapter 6

Once you have completed the MCQs above you should be ready to tackle some essay questions. You might like to select three or four topics and make notes on them. One way to do this is to create a concept map. The concept map to the first question has been done for you and you can see how the knowledge required links to some of the MCQs in this chapter.

1. In what ways do temperament approaches differ from personality approaches in the description of individual characteristics? Are there any areas of agreement between them?

2. To what extent does a better understanding of personality depend on a developmental taxonomy of higher- and lower-order traits?

3. How has behavioural genetic research played an important role in illuminating developmental processes? Explain and illustrate your answer with relevant examples.

4. Evaluate evidence in support of rank-order stability. What are the implications for the underlying assumption that personality traits in adulthood are biologically based?

5. Compare and contrast two distinct definitions of maturity that have been shown to influence development on personality.

6. Critically evaluate the implications of Carey's (2003) set-point model of personality development.

7. Critically discuss the claim that 'personality traits have no room for change from childhood to old age'.

8. Critically evaluate evidence about how personality traits shape the cultivation of social relationships.

Chapter 6 essay question 1: concept map

In what ways do temperament approaches differ from personality approaches in the description of individual characteristics? Are there any areas of agreement between them?

The concept map below provides an example of the topic areas that you might include when writing your essay. Consideration of scientific influences leads to several sub-topics that can be compared and contrasted before conclusions are drawn. Remember that it is important to link your answers to other topic areas not covered in this chapter.

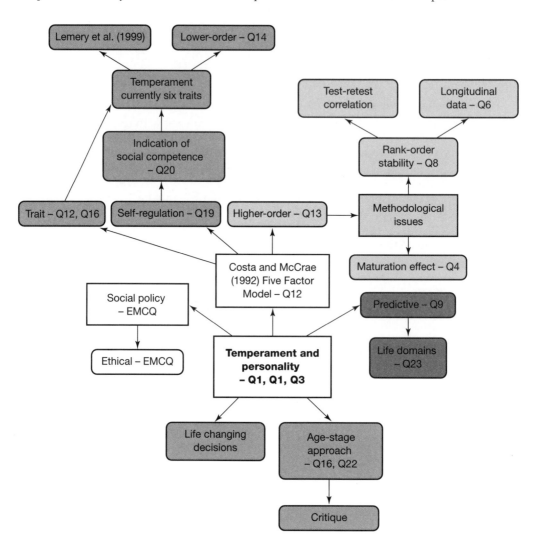

Chapter 7
Human motivation and variation

This chapter provides questions in relation to motivation and human variation. Topics include the definitions of motivation, conceptual shifts, bottom-up and top-down approaches and the link between personality and motivation.

Select one of the possible answers for each question.

Foundation level questions

1. Definitions of motivation vary. How can this impact on people's understanding of motivation?

    A. Appears to make understanding the research challenging.

    B. Appears to make understanding the research simple.

    C. It can help by influencing people's decisions.

    D. It can be difficult for younger people to understand.

    Your answer:

2. Motivation and related terms are likely to what?

    A. Be similar in academic literature and everyday use of the term(s).

    B. Differ in the academic literature and everyday use of the term(s).

    C. Be similar and different in academic use and everyday use of the term(s).

    D. None of the above.

    Your answer:

3. What can be a problem when researchers use the term motivation and related terms?

    A. Researchers can over-complicate the meaning of the term(s).

    B. Motivation and related terms to researchers only have a single meaning.

    C. Motivation and related term(s) have no meaning to researchers.

    D. The same terms can be used to mean different things.

    Your answer:

4. Which of the following is the broad purpose for the investigation of motivation?

   A. To find out how motivation functions in terms of human variation.

   B. To find out what motivation looks like from one individual to the next.

   C. To find out why people tend to behave in the way they do.

   D. To find out where motivation is.

   Your answer: ☐

5. According to Deci and Ryan (2000) what is motivation concerned with?

   A. A clear definition as an enduring trait.

   B. How to move ourselves or others to act.

   C. The identification of intelligent acts.

   D. The identification of non-intelligent acts.

   Your answer: ☐

6. The conceptualisation of motivation as self-regulation is _____ significant.

   A. Evidentially.

   B. Mostly.

   C. Theoretically.

   D. Importantly.

   Your answer: ☐

7. _____ has to some extent represented a conceptual shift in contemporary motivation research.

   A. The role of self-regulation.

   B. The role of random behaviour.

   C. The role of individual behaviour should be regulated by others which.

   D. The development of technologies.

   Your answer: ☐

Advanced level questions

8. In what way is contemporary motivation theory suggested to be best conceptualised?

    A. Only through the implicit or lay or everyday definitions people use.

    B. Through a middle of the road approach.

    C. From a top-down approach.

    D. From a bottom-up approach.

Your answer: ☐

9. What is one consequence of the conceptual shift in motivation, for researchers?

    A. Researchers' focus should be directed toward components of a top-down approach.

    B. Their focus has gone 'off track'.

    C. Researchers' focus should be directed toward components of the bottom-up approach.

    D. There is no consequence for researchers.

Your answer: ☐

10. Experiencing positive emotions has been shown to 'direct' what?

    A. General behaviour.

    B. Motivated behaviour.

    C. Honest behaviour.

    D. Enhanced behaviour.

Your answer: ☐

11. Which from the following is *not* an important motivational ingredient according to Caprara and Cervone (2000)?

    A. The Horn effect.

    B. Affective self-evaluation.

    C. Self-efficacy beliefs and perceived control.

    D. Goals and self-regulation.

Your answer: ☐

12. Effort, commitment and planning in terms of self-regulation best describe what?

A. Goals.

B. Standards.

C. Norms.

D. Affective self-evaluation.

Your answer: ☐

13. Which of the following is an overarching function of motivation?

A. To achieve dissatisfaction with one's self.

B. To a certain extent, achieve group satisfaction.

C. To achieve both self-dissatisfaction and self-satisfaction.

D. To a certain extent, achieve self-satisfaction.

Your answer: ☐

14. Historically _____ was an important concept in the early work on motivation.

A. Drive.

B. Habit.

C. Will.

D. Instinct.

Your answer: ☐

15. A key contemporary conceptual shift in motivation research has seen a rise in _____ accounts of motivation and a fall in _____ accounts.

A. Determinant, non-determinant.

B. Taxonomy, process.

C. Process, taxonomy.

D. Non-determinant, determinant.

Your answer: ☐

16. Which of the following is an important point to remember about taxonomy and process accounts of motivation?

  A. They are mutually exclusive.

  B. They are *not* mutually exclusive.

  C. They are potentially inclusive.

  D. Taxonomy and process accounts of motivation are not potentially inclusive.

Your answer: ☐

17. What are process and taxonomy accounts of motivation referred to as in the research?

  A. Bottom-up process approaches, and top-down taxonomy approaches.

  B. Bottom-up taxonomy approaches, and top-down process approaches.

  C. Underneath process approaches, over-the-top taxonomy approaches.

  D. Underneath taxonomy approaches, over-the-top process approaches.

Your answer: ☐

18. In order to encourage achievement motivation in the classroom, a student should be taught to attribute their good grades to what?

  A. Their own hard work.

  B. Their friends' hard work.

  C. Their teachers' hard work.

  D. Their outstanding intelligence.

Your answer: ☐

19. Which of the following is a top-down approach to human motivation?

  A. Einstein's (1905–16) theory of relativity.

  B. Carver and Scheier's (2000) control theory.

  C. Maslow's (1943, 1987) hierarchy of needs.

  D. Kelly's (1963) personal construct theory.

Your answer: ☐

20. Which of the following is a bottom-up approach to human motivation?

A. Maslow's (1943, 1987) hierarchy of needs.

B. Loftus and Palmer's (1974) theory of eyewitness testimony (EWT).

C. Newell's (1990) Unified Theory of Cognition.

D. Carver and Scheier's (2000) control theory.

Your answer: ☐

21. What practice do Bandura and Locke (2003) refer to as the sharing and development of theories by selecting concepts on offer within academic literature?

A. Grounded theorising.

B. Cafeteria theorising.

C. Self-regulatory theorising.

D. Cognitive theorising.

Your answer: ☐

22. Why is motivation claimed to be linked to personality?

A. Because the concepts are basically the same.

B. There is only one way to explain behaviour.

C. Because a range of psychological phenomena and processes are suggested to explain why people behave the way they do.

D. Because a range of physiological phenomena and processes are suggested to explain why people behave as they do.

Your answer: ☐

23. Self-efficacy theory draws on which of the following?

A. Social-cognitive theory.

B. Theory of planned behaviour.

C. Social identity theory.

D. Self-efficacy theory.

Your answer: ☐

24. Eysenck's and Gray's biological theories of personality are (like human motivation) concerned with?

    A. Self-importance.

    B. Self-regulation.

    C. Self-preservation.

    D. Self-report.

Your answer: ☐

Extended multiple-choice question

Identify Maslow's (1943) original five of the eight needs in Figure 7.1 using the listed items overleaf. Not all items can be used because not all items will be consistent with the figure. Items can only be used once.

Figure 7.1 An account of human motivation through Maslow's pyramid of needs

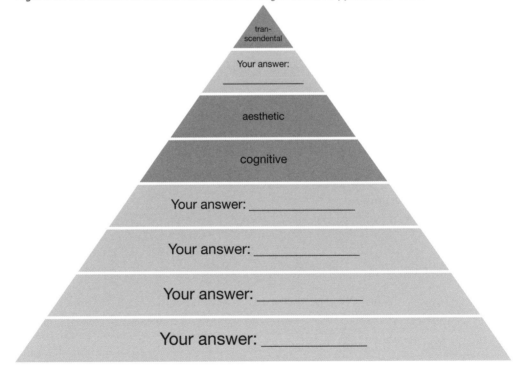

Optional items

A. warmth

B. self-actualisation

C. psychoanalytical

D. esteem

E. neuropsychological

F. belongingness and love

G. safety

H. social

I. biological and physiological

J. emotional

Essay questions for Chapter 7

Once you have completed the MCQs above you should be ready to tackle some essay questions. You might like to select three or four topics and make notes on them. One way to do this is to create a concept map. The concept map to the first question has been done for you and you can see how the knowledge required links to some of the MCQs in this chapter.

1. Critically evaluate the ways in which human personality and motivation are linked.

2. Identify and critically discuss two bottom-up approaches of human motivation.

3. Evaluate the usefulness of general self-efficacy and state self-efficacy in terms of applied theoretical and research evidence.

4. Compare and contrast two different top-down approaches to human motivation.

5. Critically evaluate competing definitions of human motivation and the implications this has for research development. Illustrate your answer with relevant examples.

6. In what ways is Maslow's (1943, 1987) account of human motivation different from Carver and Scheier's (2000a, 2000b) account of human motivation? Are there any areas of agreement between them?

7. Critically discuss the claim that human motivation is a trait and not a state. Explain and illustrate with examples.

8. In what ways do historical accounts of motivation differ from contemporary accounts of motivation? Are there any areas of agreement between them?

Chapter 7 essay question 1: concept map

Critically evaluate the ways in which human personality and motivation are linked.

The concept map below provides an example of how the first sample essay might be conceptualised. Consideration of bottom-up and top-down approaches leads to several sub-topics that can be examined for their relative strengths and weaknesses before conclusions are drawn. Remember that it is important to link your answers to other topic areas not covered in this chapter.

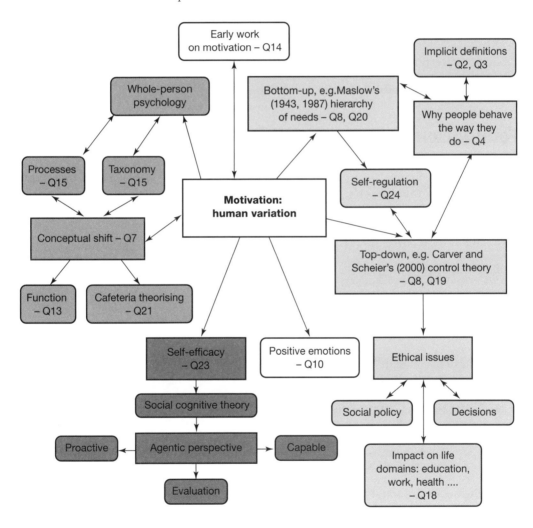

Chapter 8
Deviations: personality traits, mental health and disorder

This chapter provides questions relating to how deviations in personality traits, mental health and disorder have been linked. Topics include definitions of atypical traits, mental health and disorder, key terms and constructs, methodological considerations and prominent directions in research.

Select one of the possible answers for each question.

Foundation level questions

1. Which of the following is one way in which personality traits, mental health and disorder have been linked?

   A. Experientially.

   B. Metaphorically.

   C. Statistically.

   D. Diversely.

   Your answer:

2. Why have psychologists considered personality traits as important to mental health and disorder?

   A. Traits to some extent reflect consequences for how an individual functions.

   B. Traits to some are determinants of mental illness.

   C. Traits describe all likely mental illnesses within an individual.

   D. Because personality is the only human behaviour that can be reflected statistically in terms of mental health and disorder.

   Your answer:

3. What is an unintended consequence of the statistical link between personality traits and mental health?

A. Wild interpretations of the evidence have increased from 50% in 1990 to 100% in 2011.

B. There has been an increase in treatments and therapies for mental health and personality traits.

C. There has been a reduction in self-reports of certain traits such as neuroticism.

D. Consequences for how people manage themselves might be better described by facets or dimensions rather than traits alone.

Your answer: ☐

4. What is an important point to remember about the possible link between personality traits and mental health?

A. The link between traits and personality is causal.

B. Other constructs such as socio-economic status are likely to interact in a complex reciprocal way with traits and mental health.

C. The link between traits and personality can only be interpreted in terms of correlation coefficients.

D. Other constructs such as socio-economic status do not impact on traits and mental health.

Your answer: ☐

5. Which from the following is used to classify atypical behaviour within the UK?

A. ECT-2.

B. CSMH-1.

C. DSM-IV.

D. ICD-10.

Your answer: ☐

6. Keyes (2005; also Keyes et al., 2002) developed an approach to _____ health that accounts for both mental health and _____ that form a _____ dimension.

   A. Mental, disorder, continuous.

   B. Ill, mental, dichotomous.

   C. Flourishing, illness, continuous.

   D. Ill, disorder, categorical.

Your answer: ☐

7. In relation to mental health what is meant by the term flourishing (Keyes et al., 2002)?

   A. An adult's consistent happiness.

   B. An animal that is functioning well psychologically.

   C. A person functioning well psychologically and socially, filled with positive emotion.

   D. A group of people that functions well intellectually.

Your answer: ☐

Advanced level questions

8. Which two classification systems are predominantly used to diagnose personality disorders in Western society?

   A. SAPAS and the DSM-IVTR.

   B. DSM-IVTR and the ICD-10.

   C. ICD-10 and the SAPAS.

   D. NPI and the SAPAS.

Your answer: ☐

9. Which of the following is *not* part of Keyes's (2005) Complete State Model of Health?

   A. Mental illness and languishing.

   B. Pure languishing.

   C. Moderately mentally healthy.

   D. Significantly mentally healthy.

Your answer: ☐

10. Revelle and Scherer (2009) argue what to be a mediating factor between traits and mental health?

   A. Adaptations.

   B. Emotions.

   C. Cognitions.

   D. Rewards.

Your answer: ☐

11. Which from the following is *not* one of Johda's (1958) key features of psychological health?

   A. Negative interpersonal relations.

   B. Positive interpersonal relations.

   C. Accurate perception of reality.

   D. Environmental competence.

Your answer: ☐

12. The dark triad traits include *psychopathy, narcissism* and which other trait?

   A. Agreeableness.

   B. Machiavellianism.

   C. Neuroticism.

   D. Conscientiousness.

Your answer: ☐

13. Which Five Factor Trait is most consistently linked with all three of the dark triad?

   A. Openness.

   B. Conscientiousness.

   C. Extraversion.

   D. Agreeableness.

Your answer: ☐

14. What has research unveiled about the trait *narcissism*?

    A. The trait has a bright and dark side and has been found in clinical and non-clinical groups.

    B. Narcissism is the worst predictor out of the dark triad traits.

    C. The trait has a bright and dark side but only in clinical groups.

    D. Narcissism has no adaptive consequences for occupational groups.

Your answer: ☐

15. The use of the Five Factor Traits to diagnose personality disorders is referred to as the _____ _____.

    A. Continuity hypothesis.

    B. Discontinuity hypothesis.

    C. Yerkes hypothesis.

    D. Dodson hypothesis.

Your answer: ☐

16. How can researchers in Great Britain maintain professional and ethical standards within the individual differences psychology discipline?

    A. Through the maintenance of robust methodologies in personality research.

    B. Through adhering to government reports on research and ethical practice.

    C. By adhering to the British Psychological Society's code of conduct and ethics.

    D. By validating scientific measures of individual differences.

Your answer: ☐

17. Individuals with obsessive compulsive disorder might be treated through cognitive behavioural therapy which challenges what?

    A. Dysfunctional relationships.

    B. Dysfunctional schemata.

    C. Dysfunctional behaviour.

    D. Dysfunctional emotion.

Your answer: ☐

18. Which from the following is a frequently employed statistical technique used between traits scores and scores on measures of mental health?

A. Regression.

B. ANOVA.

C. T-tests.

D. MANOVA.

Your answer: ☐

19. Traits might indirectly or directly determine mental health and disorder. Why might this link be controversial?

A. Because of the ethical consequences for research experts in the field.

B. Because correlation coefficients determine mental health which worries experts in the field.

C. Traits can statistically predict mental health and disorder. This does not necessarily imply traits cause mental health or disorder.

D. Because research demonstrates traits do not co-vary with mental health or disorder.

Your answer: ☐

20. Why can the dark triad traits be described as atypical?

A. Because research has revealed them in both general population and clinical groups.

B. Because the traits can be linked to positive emotions.

C. The traits indicate idiosyncratic behaviours in groups and not individuals.

D. Dark triad traits are linked to personality disorder characteristics.

Your answer: ☐

Extended multiple-choice question

Complete the following paragraph using the items listed below. Not all items can be used because not all items will be consistent with the paragraph. Items can only be used once.

Recently, there has been a debate about how personality traits are linked to personality disorder. For example, typical traits such as the _____ traits can identify and diagnose personality disorder with similar accuracy to (if not better than) the classification systems such as the _____ (Tackett et al., 2009); this refers to the _____ hypothesis. It is important to develop _____ tools that can predict disorder because of the consequences for individuals' self-regulation that ultimately impacts on their well-being. However, evidence has revealed that perhaps _____ hold more useful diagnostic _____ than traits (Shelder and Westen, 2004).

Optional items

A. Five Factor

B. Big Three

C. ICD-10

D. DSM-IVTR

E. continuity

F. framework

G. accurate

H. random

I. facets

J. value

Essay questions for Chapter 8

Once you have completed the MCQs above you should be ready to tackle some essay questions. You might like to select three or four topics and make notes on them. One way to do this is to create a concept map. The concept map for the first question has been done for you and you can see how the knowledge required links to some of the MCQs in this chapter.

1. In what ways do dark triad traits differ from Five Factor Traits in the explanation of mental disorder? Are there any areas of agreement between them?

2. Critically examine how atypical personality traits have been defined. What are the implications of atypical definitions?

3. Why can mental health (particularly within the UK) not be understood unless it is considered with mental disorder?

4. To what extent does a link between personality traits and mental health depend on the functional definition of behaviour?

5. What are the basic assumptions about personality disorder? How are these reflected by the Five Factor Model?

6. Evaluate evidence in support of biological theories of mental disorder. What are the implications for the medical model of mental disorder?

7. Compare and contrast the ethical and professional issues faced by expert practitioners and expert researchers when working (in the UK) with the complex links between typical and atypical personality.

8. Discuss, critically, the assertion that 'personality traits are indicators of mental health'.

Chapter 8 essay question 1: concept map

In what ways do dark triad traits differ from Five Factor Traits in the explanation of mental disorder? Are there any areas of agreement between them?

The concept map below provides an example of how the first essay might be conceptualised. You might compare and contrast key features of each trait model before moving on to analysing theoretical and research evidence. This organised approach should lead you to a sound conclusion in relation to the set question. Remember other topic areas not covered in this chapter can be linked to your answer too.

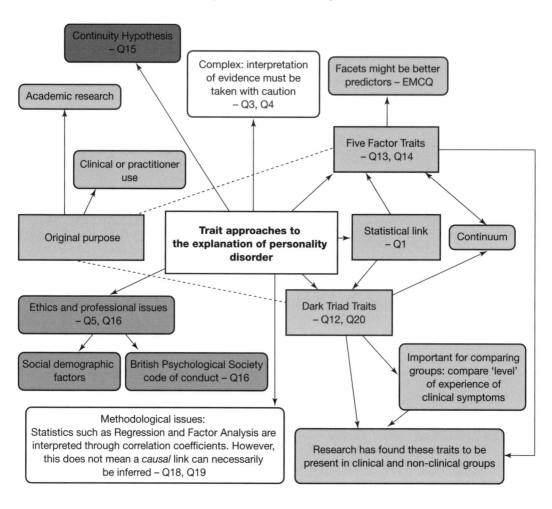

Chapter 9
Moving forward: individual differences psychology

This chapter provides questions relating to how individual differences psychology is moving forward in relation to research and theory about human variation. The chapter includes topics such as contributions to our understanding of human variation, partial progress in the field and the challenges ahead for individual differences psychology.

Select one of the possible answers for each question.

Foundation level questions

1. According to Boyle and Saklofske (2004) individual differences psychology should acknowledge what?

   A. Human psychological variations are static processes.

   B. Human psychological variations are stationary processes.

   C. Human psychological variations are dynamic processes.

   D. Human psychological variations are non-existent.

   Your answer: ☐

2. Which of the following describes an implicit assumption?

   A. Lay assumption.

   B. Theoretical assumption.

   C. Formal scientific assumption.

   D. Grandiose assumption.

   Your answer: ☐

3. Which of the following best describes systematic similarities or differences that appear to typify an individual's or group of individuals' behaviour, thoughts and feelings?

A. A person's soul.

B. A person's religion.

C. Enduring characteristics.

D. A connection between people.

Your answer: ☐

4. How has the relationship between the person and situation variables been seen?

A. Simple and unidirectional.

B. Complex and unidirectional.

C. Simple and reciprocal.

D. Complex and reciprocal.

Your answer: ☐

5. One _____ over earlier perspectives is the general recognition that personality develops and _____ through the reciprocal interaction with the _____ environment (Bandura, 1986).

A. Relapse, processes, biological.

B. Advance, functions, sociocultural.

C. Retreat, progresses, physical.

D. Advance, functions, physical.

Your answer: ☐

6. Which of the following is an encouraging development for phenotypic inter-individual differences?

A. A five-factor structure of personality.

B. A one-factor structure of personality.

C. Genetic variance.

D. Explaining random error.

Your answer: ☐

7. What is a reason for optimism about social-cognitive theory in terms of personality?

   A. The central tenet that people do not contribute to their course of development.

   B. Wider recognition that people contribute proactively to their course of development.

   C. Social-cognitive theory is unlikely to provide a complete theory of personality.

   D. Social-cognitive theory has already provided a complete theory of personality.

   Your answer: ☐

Advanced level questions

8. What would be one benefit for an investigator who examines personality scientifically?

   A. Not to bother because it is too complex to fully investigate personality scientifically.

   B. Pay less attention on causal mechanisms of personality.

   C. Greater emphasis on identifying causal mechanisms.

   D. Greater emphasis on bigger correlation coefficients.

   Your answer: ☐

9. Why should individual differences psychology focus on whole-person psychology?

   A. To present psychologists with a challenge.

   B. To provide an empty understanding of individual differences.

   C. To be 'more scientific'.

   D. To provide the fullest understanding of individual differences.

   Your answer: ☐

10. According to Yanchar et al. (2008) what is a more pressing focus for the future development of individual differences psychology?

    A. Implicit theoretical assumptions of the field.

    B. Formal academic definitions within the field.

    C. Implicit theoretical definitions of the field.

    D. None of the above.

    Your answer: ☐

11. Which of the following is one issue with a theory that posits both a biological and environmental determinism on an individual's variation?

A. There is little room left for a social cognitive account of the individual's variation.

B. There is little room left that accounts for the free will of an individual.

C. The public tends not to like these theories.

D. These theories are too heavily based on implicit assumptions.

Your answer: ☐

12. Which from the following is *not* one of McAdams and Pals' (2006) principles for an integrative science of personality?

A. Evolution and human nature.

B. Characteristic adaptations.

C. The differential role of culture.

D. The differential role of animal nature.

Your answer: ☐

13. What is the credibility of individual differences psychology currently reliant upon?

A. The credibility of individual differences psychologists.

B. The credibility of individuals.

C. The credibility of its methods.

D. A complete disregard for the psychoanalytic approach.

Your answer: ☐

14. Why is it suggested to be unlikely that an ultimate theoretical framework of personality will be solely biologically based?

A. Because of the individual's processes of meaning construction and self-reflection.

B. Because biology will not be able to uncover causal mechanisms of human variation.

C. Biology does not consider physiological aspects of personality.

D. Biology accounts only for the functions of human variation and not the structure.

Your answer: ☐

15. Metcalfe and Mischel's (1999) hot/cool cognition framework has highlighted what in terms of individual differences?

   A. A revolution in psychology.

   B. A weakness in the psychometric approach.

   C. A conceptual framework developed outside the mainstream of psychometrics.

   D. Whole-person psychology is all about cognition and not personality.

Your answer: ☐

16. Previously it could have been argued that challenging mainstream ideas of individual differences psychology was difficult because …

   A. Many research publications fail to report null findings.

   B. Many research publications report null findings as well as significant results.

   C. Statistically significant results are not reported in the research.

   D. None of the above.

Your answer: ☐

17. What is McCrae's (2004) proposition for linking personality and culture?

   A. A personality system based on a biopsychosocial framework.

   B. A personality system based on a biomedical framework.

   C. A personality system based on childhood experiences.

   D. A personality system developed by culture alone.

Your answer: ☐

18. Why is McCrae's (2004) theoretical framework to some degree controversial?

   A. The theory does not account for genetic influence.

   B. Because of the causality assumption implied that personality trait affects culture.

   C. The theory does not account for developmental influence.

   D. Because the theory is not specific enough.

Your answer: ☐

19. Which of the following has only provided evidence *against* the 'universality' of personality across cultures?

    A. Universal causality → biological and genetic basis of personality traits.

    B. Universal structure → different sociocultural contexts.

    C. Trait intensity patterns.

    D. Lifespan stability.

    Your answer: ☐

20. Broadly, what is demonstrated by the evidence about personality traits and culture?

    A. Cultures do not vary in their main trait profiles.

    B. No discernable patterns have been made about culture and personality.

    C. The personality-culture link is similar.

    D. Cultures vary in their mean trait profiles.

    Your answer: ☐

Extended multiple-choice question

Complete Boxes 1 and 5 in Figure 9.1, then complete the paragraph opposite. Remember not all items will be consistent with the diagram or paragraph. Items can only be used once.

Figure 9.1 McAdams and Pals' (2006, p213) Five Principles of Personality Psychology

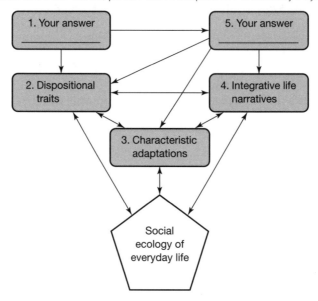

Broadly speaking the _____ of individual differences psychology is somewhat entwined with a scientific basis in unravelling human _____ and uniqueness. Indeed this is a _____ quality of individual differences psychology. However, Yanchar et al. (2008) have suggested that scientific analytic reasoning needs to be set behind the _____ acknowledgement of implicit theoretical assumptions. Thus a key _____ for the future is _____ thinking that is transparent throughout the discipline of individual differences psychology.

Optional items

A. culture

B. research

C. credibility

D. human nature

E. individuality

F. social

G. reflective

H. development

I. human nuture

J. critical

K. orginal

L. distinctive

Essay questions for Chapter 9

Once you have completed the MCQs above you should be ready to tackle some essay questions. You might like to select three or four topics and make notes on them. One way to do this is to create a concept map. The concept map for the first question has been done for you and you can see how the knowledge required links to some of the MCQs in this chapter.

1. 'No present concept of personality will survive the next half century' (Kagan, 1998, p198). To what extent do you agree with this view?

2. Examine critically the claim that 'the credibility of individual differences psychology is tied to psychometric methods'.

3. To what extent has theory and research on intelligence begun to take an integrated approach to human variation?

4. Evaluate evidence in support of theories of an integrative science of personality. What are the implications for the whole-person approach to human variation?

5. How have changes to the way in which human psychological variation should be conceptualised affected research on personality? Illustrate your answer with relevant examples.

6. Evaluate the strengths and weaknesses of theories and research that link personality to culture.

7. Critically evaluate the negative consequences of individual differences research in relation to one of the following main topic areas: personality; motivation; intelligence.

8. Examine the claim that 'critical thinking within individual differences psychology cannot be fully understood unless it involves identifying implicit theoretical assumptions'.

Chapter 9 essay question 1: concept map

'No present concept of personality will survive the next half century' (Kagan, 1998, p198). To what extent do you agree with this view?

The concept map below provides an example of how the first sample essay might be conceptualised. Consideration of the scientific influence in individual differences psychology leads to several sub-topics that can be examined for their relative strengths and weaknesses before conclusions are drawn. Remember that it is important to link your answers to other topic areas not covered in this chapter.

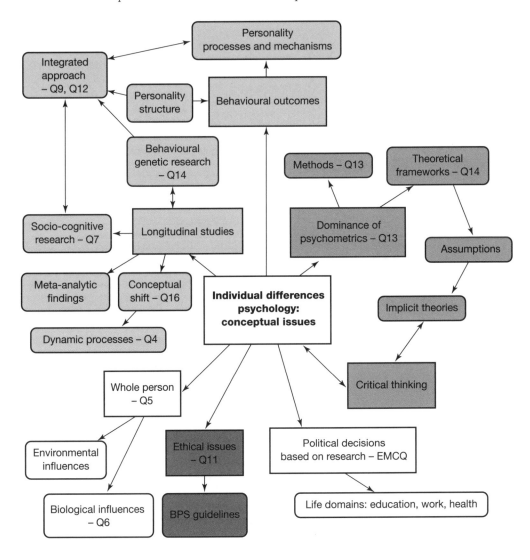

Writing an essay: a format for success

After answering the questions in this book you have probably become more aware of the vast landscape individual differences psychology encompasses. The multiple-choice questions within this revision text are by no means exhaustive – far from it. The book is a mere whistle-stop tour of some of the elements that make up individual differences psychology. Hence, to pin down a format for success when writing an individual-differences psychology essay presents a challenge even to the most prepared essay writer. Therefore to be able to answer and apply the question 'What are the more distinctive elements of an individual differences psychology essay?', a good starting place is to identify essential criteria of a more general essay format, as shown in the diagram below.

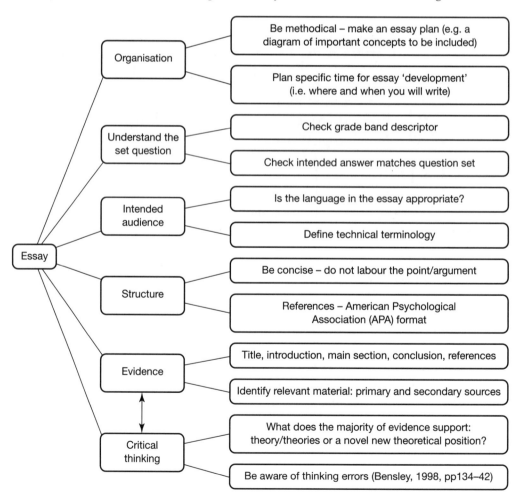

The diagram identifies references as essential to your essay. Broadly, this is because references provide a way to structure evidence and prevent the writer (you) from plagiarism (i.e. palming the work of others off as your own). APA reference format can be found at: http://owl.english.purdue.edu/owl/resource/560/01/.

Primary evidence (e.g. journals, government reports, video diaries, etc.) and secondary evidence (e.g. books, systematic reviews, meta-analyses) are two key sources of evidence within a more successful essay (Redman, 2001). Primary and secondary sources of evidence are important because they add 'weight' to an argument by support or refutation of a claim. The synthesis of primary and secondary evidence provides you with the opportunity to express your method of reasoning (inductive or/and deductive), as Bensley (1998, p5) suggests:

> *Critical thinking is reflective thinking involving the evaluation of evidence relevant to a claim so that a sound conclusion can be drawn from the evidence.*

This is a 'working definition' of critical thinking which will aid your approach to an essay question. Now we can identify specific essential criteria for an individual differences psychology essay which can be synthesised into themes. That is, when answering a set essay question it is important to account for the following aspects:

- Consider the 'nature/nurture' debate. The essay must consider how the set essay question can be analysed in terms of the relative influences of inherited and environmental factors (Penke et al., 2007). These influences underlie the main topic areas of individual differences such as intelligence, personality and motivation, and therefore influence to some extent the direction of enquiry.

- Psychometrics is currently the predominant approach to individual differences psychology (Bartram and Lindley, 2005). Therefore you should discuss the strengths and weaknesses of such an approach in relation to the set question because of the conceptual, methodological and practical implications that underlie this approach.

- You might consider social sensitivity because individual differences research and theory can influence a particular political stance (Boyle and Saklofske, 2004). Therefore significant decisions made based on individual differences psychology evidence must account for the actual or potential implications that impact on individuals or/and groups as well as society at large, in terms of social policy.

A final point is that ethical consideration is a strongly recommended theme of an essay in psychology. This means you must be reflective in your communication of how the evidence relevant to a claim impacts on those that are researched and the practical and professional implications for the researcher(s). Beauchamp and Childress's (1989) useful rubric of 'four cardinal principles' that overarch ethical considerations for research might be a good starting point for your enquiry into ethics and research.

References

Bartram, D. and Lindley, P. (2005) *Psychological testing: the BPS Test Administration (Occupational) Open Learning Programme*. Oxford: BPS Blackwell.

Beauchamp, T.L. and Childress, J. F. (1989) *Principles of biomedical ethics* (3rd edn). Oxford: Oxford University Press. (First published 1979).

Bensley, D.A. (1998) *Critical thinking in psychology: a unified skills approach*. Pacific Grove, CA: Brooks/Cole Publishing Company.

Boyle, G.J. and Saklofske, D.H. (2004) (eds) *Sage benchmarks in psychology: psychology of individual differences*. London: Sage.

Penke, L., Denissen, J.J.A. and Miller, G.F. (2007) The evolutionary genetics of personality. *European Journal of Personality*, 21, 549-587.

Redman, P. (2001) *Good essay writing: a social sciences guide* (2nd edn). London: Sage Publications.

Scoring methods
in MCQs

Introduction

All assessments need to be reviewed and marked. At your university you will come across a number of formal (often called summative) and informal (aka formative) assessments. These can take the form of practical reports, essays, short-answer questions and (of course) examinations. There are, of course, a number of forms of examinations – short answers, written essays and multiple-choice questions (or MCQs).

MCQs are considered objective assessments, that is answers are unambiguously correct or incorrect and therefore provide for high marker reliability – so that's one positive mark for MCQs. On the other hand, there is often a concern (for the examination setter) that guessing by the candidate can have an inflationary influence on the marks. By chance, if you have four choices then you should score 25% just by guessing. This is obviously not a situation to be encouraged, and because of this your psychology course team may have introduced various attempts to make sure that this does not happen. It is worth exploring some of these methods and the implications these will have for the approach you take to your assessment and, ultimately, how they can impact on your examination performance.

Scoring of MCQ examinations can take several forms. At its most simple, a raw score is calculated based on the total number of correct responses (usually 1 mark per correct answer). Under this approach, any omissions or incorrect responses earn you no marks but neither do they attract a penalty. If you get the question right, you get a mark; if you do not then you get no mark.

As mentioned, alternative and more complex approaches to marking have been developed because of concerns that results can be inflated if correct responses are the result of successful guessing. The most common approaches to discouraging random guessing include the reward of partial knowledge and negative marking. This can impact on your behaviour and your learning. Of course, whatever the examination and whatever the marking scheme, you need to know your stuff!

Rewarding partial knowledge

Scoring procedures developed to reward partial knowledge are based on the assumption that though you and your student colleagues may be unable to identify a single correct response you can confidently identify some options as being incorrect and that partial knowledge should therefore be rewarded. Versions of this approach generally allow you to choose:

- more than one possibly correct response and to be awarded a partial mark provided one of your responses is the correct answer;
- a 'not sure' option for which you are awarded a proportion of a mark (usually either 0.2 or 0.25).

Negative marking

Negative marking is when your performance is based on the total number of correct responses which is then reduced in some way to correct for any potential guessing. The simplest application of negative marking is where equal numbers of marks are added or subtracted for right and wrong answers and omitted answers or the selection of a 'No answer' option that has no impact on marks. So, you get +1 mark when you get the question right, –1 mark when you get it wrong and 0 if you do not attempt it. However, there are other approaches which are slightly more punitive. In these approaches, if you get the question correct you get +1, if you get the question wrong then this is awarded a –1 (or even –2) and if there is no attempt then this is awarded a –1 as well as, it is suggested, you do not know the answer.

How does this impact on you?

The impact of these scoring mechanisms can be significant. By way of example, use the following table to demonstrate your performance in each of the chapters in this text. For each of the chapters work out the number of correct responses (and code this as NC), the number of incorrect answers (coded as NI) and the number of questions that you did not provide a response to (NR). You can then use the formulae in the table to work out how you would have performed under each of the different marking schemes. For example, for the punitive negative marking scheme you score 18 correct (NC=18), 2 incorrect (NI=2) and omitted 5 questions (NR=5). On the basis of the formula in the table, NC-(NI*2)-NR, you would have scored 9 (i.e. 18-(2*2)-5). So even though you managed to get 18 out of 25 this would have been reduced to only 9 because of the punitive marking.

Chapter	Number correct	Number incorrect	No response	Marking scheme: raw score	Marking scheme: partial knowledge	Marking scheme: negative marking	Marking scheme: punitive negative marking
	NC	NI	NR	$= NC$	$= NC - (NI * 0.2)$	$= NC - NI$	$= NC - (NI * 2) - NR$
1							
2							
3							
4							
5							
6							
7							
8							
9							
TOTAL							

Explore the scores above – which chapter did you excel at and for which chapter do you need to do some work? Use the above table to see your areas of strength and areas of weakness – and consequently where you need to spend more time revising and reviewing the material.

MCQ answers

Chapter 1: Individual differences psychology: a brief introduction – MCQ answers

Level	Question number	Correct response	Self-monitoring
Foundation	1	D	
Foundation	2	D	
Foundation	3	B	
Foundation	4	C	
Foundation	5	D	
Foundation	6	B	
Foundation	7	B	
Advanced	8	B	
Advanced	9	C	
Advanced	10	A	
Advanced	11	D	
Advanced	12	D	
Advanced	13	D	
Advanced	14	B	
Advanced	15	B	
Advanced	16	C	
Advanced	17	B	
Advanced	18	A	
Advanced	19	B	
Advanced	20	C	
Advanced	21	A	
Advanced	22	A	
Advanced	23	D	
Advanced	24	A	
Advanced	25	D	
Advanced	26	A	
		Total number of points:	Foundation: Advanced:

EMCQ for Chapter 1

The paragraph should read as follows. A maximum of 7 points can be awarded.

The scientific measurement of <u>enduring</u> dispositions is a predominant focus within the field of individual differences psychology. This is partly because <u>dispositions</u> or characteristics that typify people are assumed to represent meaning and therefore have consequences for individuals and groups. A feature of this <u>systematic</u> approach is it provides scientists with a <u>comparative</u> <u>standard</u> with other members of the population, which can be applied through valid and <u>reliable</u> instruments. However, scoring and interpretation are complex, and include ethical as well as development and <u>administrative</u> challenges in the application of individual differences measures. Consequently, a call for an <u>integrated</u> approach to individual differences has been made as part of an effort to consolidate a whole-person approach to the field.

Chapter 2: Personality: evolutionary, physiological and trait approaches – MCQ answers

Level	Question number	Correct response	Self-monitoring
Foundation	1	A	
Foundation	2	D	
Foundation	3	C	
Foundation	4	D	
Foundation	5	B	
Foundation	6	A	
Foundation	7	A	
Advanced	8	B	
Advanced	9	C	
Advanced	10	B	
Advanced	11	A	
Advanced	12	C	
Advanced	13	D	
Advanced	14	A	
Advanced	15	C	
Advanced	16	A	
Advanced	17	B	
Advanced	18	C	
Advanced	19	B	
Advanced	20	B	
Advanced	21	D	
Advanced	22	A	
		Total number of points:	Foundation: Advanced:

EMCQ for Chapter 2

The paragraph should read as follows. A maximum of 10 points can be awarded.

There is a wealth of evidence that supports the Five <u>Factor</u> Model of personality. For example, the factor constructs have been <u>reliably</u> identified in various cultures and languages through self and peer reports (Caprara and Cervone, 2000); the biological indicators of some of the traits, that is the <u>variability</u> between scores on personality inventories, have shown physiological <u>differences</u> between individuals. There remains apprehension in concluding that these factors will have an <u>enduring</u> role in a <u>scientific</u> theory of personality (ibid.). This is partly because of the kinds of studies the FFM produces which often identify and describe how two things <u>co-occur</u>, for example the variance of a student's conscientiousness score and the <u>correlation</u> this has with their mathematics exam score. Thus there is no <u>causal</u> link that is explained in this research. Therefore, while the FFM describes the structure of personality, there remains space for a functional integrative theory to better understand and <u>explain</u> personality.

Chapter 3: Genetics and environment: a view of individuality and uniqueness – MCQ answers

Level	Question number	Correct response	Self-monitoring
Foundation	1	B	
Foundation	2	C	
Foundation	3	A	
Foundation	4	B	
Foundation	5	D	
Foundation	6	A	
Foundation	7	C	
Foundation	8	C	
Foundation	9	A	
Foundation	10	C	
Advanced	11	A	
Advanced	12	B	
Advanced	13	D	
Advanced	14	D	
Advanced	15	D	
Advanced	16	B	
Advanced	17	A	
Advanced	18	B	
Advanced	19	D	
Advanced	20	D	
Advanced	21	A	
Advanced	22	C	
		Total number of points:	Foundation: Advanced:

EMCQ 1 for Chapter 3

Figure 3.1 should read as follows. A maximum of 5 points can be awarded.

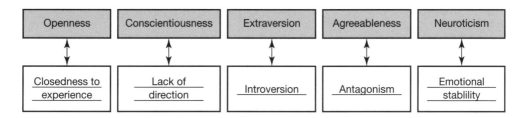

EMCQ 2 for Chapter 3

Figure 3.2 should read as follows: A maximum of 9 points can be awarded

Openness	Extraversion	Agreeableness
• Ideas	• Warmth	• Trust
• Actions	• Activity	• Modesty
• Aesthetics	• Assertiveness	• Altruism

Chapter 4: Personality: *a reflection on physcial health – MCQ answers*

Level	Question number	Correct response	Self-monitoring
Foundation	1	A	
Foundation	2	B	
Foundation	3	D	
Foundation	4	C	
Foundation	5	A	
Foundation	6	D	
Foundation	7	A	
Advanced	8	C	
Advanced	9	C	
Advanced	10	B	
Advanced	11	A	
Advanced	12	A	
Advanced	13	C	
Advanced	14	B	
Advanced	15	A	
Advanced	16	A	
Advanced	17	B	
Advanced	18	C	
Advanced	19	A	
Advanced	20	D	
Advanced	21	A	
Advanced	22	C	
Advanced	23	B	
Advanced	24	A	
		Total number of points:	Foundation: Advanced:

EMCQ for Chapter 4

The paragraph should read as follows. A maximum of 9 points can be awarded.

There has been a lengthy precedence of the link between personality, <u>physical</u> <u>health</u> and disease processes. A key premise is that <u>psychological</u> factors are implicated with individual differences in the recovery and possibly the <u>onset</u> of physical health or disease. For example, Friedman and Rosenman (1959) were able to relate processes of cardiovascular disease with certain behaviour patterns in middle-aged men; this link has been described as Type <u>A</u> behaviour pattern (TABP) with <u>opposite</u> behaviours described as Type <u>B</u> behaviour pattern. However, the link between TABP and cardiovascular disease has been questioned on the grounds of <u>method</u> dependency. Nevertheless, there is compelling evidence that TABP can predict the likely onset of <u>cardiovascular</u> disease (Lachar, 1993). An important focus to come from this research is the link between <u>emotion</u> and behaviour that mediates personality and physical health (ibid.).

Chapter 5: Intelligence and individual differences – MCQ answers

Level	Question number	Correct response	Self-monitoring
Foundation	1	D	
Foundation	2	A	
Foundation	3	A	
Foundation	4	C	
Foundation	5	A	
Foundation	6	B	
Foundation	7	D	
Advanced	8	B	
Advanced	9	A	
Advanced	10	B	
Advanced	11	C	
Advanced	12	A	
Advanced	13	C	
Advanced	14	C	
Advanced	15	C	
Advanced	16	B	
Advanced	17	A	
Advanced	18	B	
Advanced	19	D	
Advanced	20	D	
Advanced	21	A	
Advanced	22	B	
Advanced	23	D	
Advanced	24	C	
Advanced	25	C	
Advanced	26	A	
Advanced	27	B	
Advanced	28	A	
		Total number of points:	Foundation: Advanced:

EMCQ for Chapter 5

The paragraph should read as follows. A maximum of 7 points can be awarded.

The use and <u>interpretation</u> of intellectual ability tests by academics and non-academics have far-reaching <u>consequences</u> for people. For example, a controversy was unleashed when the possible link between race and IQ was made by Jensen (1969), who suggested black people have innately lower IQs because on average their scores were lower than whites on the same standardised intellectual ability test. However, this research is flawed from a genetic perspective as we cannot suggest there is more genetic <u>variation</u> in one racial group than <u>between</u> racial groups. Therefore socio-political <u>implications</u> are of central relevance in the prevention of potential or <u>actual</u> misrepresented use and interpretation of explicit <u>standardised</u> tests.

Chapter 6: Personality development across the lifespan – MCQ answers

Level	Question number	Correct response	Self-monitoring
Foundation	1	C	
Foundation	2	A	
Foundation	3	C	
Foundation	4	B	
Foundation	5	A	
Foundation	6	D	
Foundation	7	D	
Advanced	8	D	
Advanced	9	C	
Advanced	10	A	
Advanced	11	D	
Advanced	12	C	
Advanced	13	B	
Advanced	14	C	
Advanced	15	A	
Advanced	16	C	
Advanced	17	A	
Advanced	18	A	
Advanced	19	B	
Advanced	20	C	
Advanced	21	D	
Advanced	22	D	
Advanced	23	C	
Advanced	24	B	
		Total number of points:	Foundation: Advanced:

EMCQ for Chapter 6

The paragraph should read as follows. A maximum of 8 points can be awarded.

Research on cognitive <u>development</u> indicates that IQ heritability estimates <u>increase</u> from early childhood through to late adolescence (Plomin et al., 1997). Thus the balance of genetic versus <u>environmental</u> influences varies at successive developmental 'stages'. Findings also suggest that 'shared environmental' factors have less <u>influence</u> on the effect of IQ between siblings as they age which has been attributed to the fact that siblings increasingly seek out environments <u>correlated</u> with their own genetic endowments. However, <u>professionals</u> must be acutely aware of the high-level <u>decision-making</u> that at times accompanies the interpretation of such results which is a key reason for taking a <u>critical thinking</u> stance toward personality outcomes and lifespan development research (Yanchar et al., 2008).

Chapter 7: Human motivation and variation – MCQ answers

Level	Question number	Correct response	Self-monitoring
Foundation	1	A	
Foundation	2	B	
Foundation	3	D	
Foundation	4	C	
Foundation	5	B	
Foundation	6	C	
Foundation	7	A	
Advanced	8	D	
Advanced	9	C	
Advanced	10	C	
Advanced	11	A	
Advanced	12	A	
Advanced	13	D	
Advanced	14	A	
Advanced	15	C	
Advanced	16	B	
Advanced	17	A	
Advanced	18	A	
Advanced	19	C	
Advanced	20	D	
Advanced	21	B	
Advanced	22	C	
Advanced	23	A	
Advanced	24	B	
		Total number of points:	Foundation: Advanced:

EMCQ for Chapter 7

Figure 7.1 should read as follows. A maximum of 5 points can be awarded.

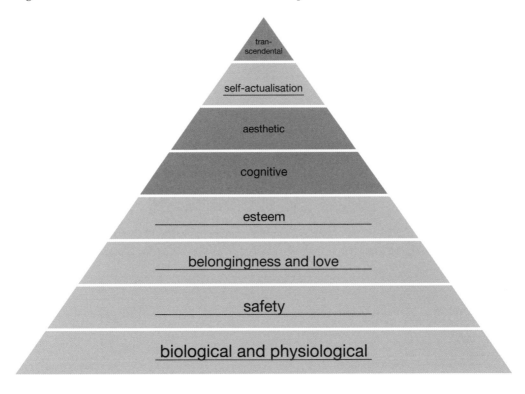

Chapter 8: Deviations: personality traits, mental health and disorder – MCQ answers

Level	Question number	Correct response	Self-monitoring
Foundation	1	C	
Foundation	2	A	
Foundation	3	D	
Foundation	4	B	
Foundation	5	D	
Foundation	6	A	
Foundation	7	C	
Advanced	8	D	
Advanced	9	B	
Advanced	10	A	
Advanced	11	B	
Advanced	12	A	
Advanced	13	D	
Advanced	14	A	
Advanced	15	A	
Advanced	16	C	
Advanced	17	B	
Advanced	18	A	
Advanced	19	C	
Advanced	20	D	
		Total number of points:	Foundation: Advanced:

EMCQ for Chapter 8

The paragraph should read as follows. A maximum of 6 points can be awarded.

Recently, there has been a debate about how personality traits are linked to personality disorder. For example, typical traits such as the <u>Five Factor</u> traits can identify and diagnose personality disorder with similar accuracy to (if not better than) the classification systems such as the <u>ICD-10</u> (Tackett et al., 2009); this refers to the <u>continuity</u> hypothesis. It is important to develop <u>accurate</u> tools that can predict disorder because of the consequences for individuals' self-regulation that ultimately impacts on their well-being. However, evidence has revealed that perhaps <u>facets</u> hold more useful diagnostic <u>value</u> than traits (Shelder and Westen, 2004).

Chapter 9: Moving forward: individual differences psychology – MCQ answers

Level	Question number	Correct response	Self-monitoring
Foundation	1	C	
Foundation	2	A	
Foundation	3	C	
Foundation	4	D	
Foundation	5	B	
Foundation	6	A	
Foundation	7	B	
Advanced	8	C	
Advanced	9	D	
Advanced	10	A	
Advanced	11	B	
Advanced	12	A	
Advanced	13	C	
Advanced	14	A	
Advanced	15	C	
Advanced	16	A	
Advanced	17	A	
Advanced	18	B	
Advanced	19	D	
Advanced	20	D	
		Total number of points:	Foundation: Advanced:

EMCQ for Chapter 9

Figure 9.1 should read as follows. A maximum of 2 points can be awarded.

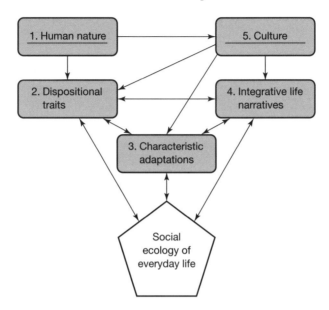

The paragraph should read as follows. A maximum of 6 points can be awarded.

Broadly speaking the <u>credibility</u> of individual differences psychology is somewhat entwined with a scientific basis in unravelling human <u>individuality</u> and uniqueness. Indeed this is a <u>distinctive</u> quality of individual differences psychology. However, Yanchar et al. (2008) have suggested that scientific analytic reasoning needs to be set behind the <u>reflective</u> acknowledgement of implicit theoretical assumptions. Thus a key <u>development</u> for the future is <u>critical</u> thinking that is transparent throughout the discipline of individual differences psychology.